MW00640600

CRYSTAL STAIRS, Inc.

Due North!
Strengthen Your LEADERSHIP Assets™

11/23/02

Sheila —

You are one
phenomenal sister!
All the best as you
continue your leadership
journey. The amazing
story of meeting Zhanda
continues to validate the
network working.
Keep climbing!
Zyla

Due North!

Due North!

STRENGTHEN YOUR LEADERSHIP ASSETS™

Jylla Moore Foster

Crystal Stairs Publishers
Hinsdale, IL

A hardcover edition of this book was published in 2002 by Crystal Stairs Publishers.

Copyright © 2002 Jylla Moore Foster

All rights reserved. No part of this book may be reproduced or transmitted in any form or by any means, electronic or mechanical, including photocopying, recording, or by any information storage and retrieval system, without written permission from the publisher. For information, contact Crystal Stairs Publishers, P. O. Box 157, Hinsdale, IL 60521
DueNorth@Crystal-Stairs.com
www.Crystal-Stairs.com

Crystal Stairs Publishers titles may be purchased for business or promotional use or for special sales. For information, please contact Crystal Stairs Publishers.

ISBN 0-9722441-0-7
    Publisher's Cataloging-in-Publication Data
Foster, Jylla Moore.
        Due North! : strengthen your leadership assets / by Jylla Moore Foster.
    —Burr Ridge, IL : Crystal Stairs, 2002.

        p. ; cm.

    Includes bibliographical references.
    ISBN 0-9722441-0-7
        1. Leadership. 2. Self-actualization (Psychology). 3. Self-confidence.
    4. Self-management (Psychology). 5. Success. I. Title.

BF637.L4 F67 2002   2002110720
158.4—dc21   0210

06 05 04 03 02 • 5 4 3 2 1

Book Coordination by Jenkins Group, Inc. • www.bookpublishing.com
Printed in the United States of America

To my phenomenal mother, Vera Moore,
my Soror and my friend
who has provided a lifetime of unconditional love.

To my father, Julius Moore Sr.,
who left this world too early
to witness and enjoy the fruits of his love and labor.

To my daughter, Anjylla,
for keeping my spirit young and adventuresome.

To my family, friends, and colleagues . . .
past, present, and future,

I am *truly blessed* and *grateful*!

— *Jylla Moore Foster*

CONTENTS

INTRODUCTION

All that you do, do with your might.
Things done by half are never done right.

JULIUS AND VERA MOORE
Dad and Mom

I always receive a lot of energy and learn a lot whenever I have the opportunity to spend time with my daughter and other children. While on a camping trip with her class at White Pines Ranch: A dude ranch just for kids!, I attended an "Orienteering" class in which I learned the four steps to finding your direction with a compass. As the group leader explained, the first step is to point yourself in the direction of north.

"Plug it in to your body," she said, holding the compass close to her chest. "Put red Fred in the shed, find a landmark in the direction you want to travel, and go!"

If we can calibrate our "Work/Life Equation" in such a way that we keep our eyes focused on our landmarks and carry a toolkit of assets that can be used at any fork in the road, then we can plot our way north. With our compass pointed due north, we will find the way to success, the same way our ancestors used the North Star to find their way to freedom, new possibilities, and new opportunities. In which direction is your compass pointed?

DUE NORTH! Strengthen Your Leadership Assets™ is an invitation to embark on a leadership journey. These *Leadership Assets*™, critical both to your personal and professional lives, are as applicable to seasoned corporate executives as they are to new entrants to the work force. They can help entrepreneurs, leaders of organizations, small and multibillion-dollar businesses, the public and the private sectors, students matriculating in schools, and adults with lifelong learning plans. They are transferable assets to use at life's crossroads, blind spots, and roadblocks. This book will guide you in making flexible choices, adapting plans, and choosing creative courses of action.

This book also is about the value of coaching and the difference it can make in the direction of your life, business, or organization. Today, many individuals and businesses engage coaches to drive personal and professional results. A coach provides an action-oriented support system for individuals and groups to clarify objectives, to focus and actualize goals. Coaching is a process of probing, requesting, and challenging. You examine and rethink actions. You focus on what *really* matters and objectively assess competencies. You discover your own truths and map out a plan by which to live. The "Coach Approach" bridges the gap between your reality and dreams while facilitating the changes you want or need to make. By sharing my experiences and those of my clients in this book, coaching is transformed from theory to action.

➤ Climbing the corporate ladder . . .
➤ Going up the down escalator . . .
➤ Ascending to greater heights in an organization . . .
➤ Mapping your amazing personal journey . . .

When we embark upon a journey, we move along the road that is closest to our comfort zone and has the fewest roadblocks. We plot the quickest route and the fastest path. We move without a clear sense of purpose to propel our momentum.

The laser questioning of the coaching process can illuminate your steps and help you navigate your direction. As you proceed, shifts will likely occur. You will respond to the power of divine intervention and yield to coachable moments in your life as you navigate your future. You will be encouraged to stop for a few coffee breaks along the way and even take the scenic route so that you can breathe fresh air and appreciate the true beauty of the trip.

Embracing the shifts that we confront in life requires our personal focus and commitment to living in a *conscious* and *intentional* manner. This book contains 12 Leadership Assets™ that provide the roadmap. You cannot call AAA for a Trip-Tik. You can't search MapQuest® for directions. You can't inspect a cruise itinerary or check an airline's Internet fares. Using this book as your guide, you will have to plot your own path. I promise you it will be an amazing journey.

Explore the contents and assess your road-readiness. My stories, coachable moments, and the Coach Approach are the mile-markers on the journey to professional development and personal transformation. They can help you create and execute your plan.

My fortitude, my energy, my strength, my life's work, my passion is helping people find their way with the assistance of the Crystal Stairs Leadership Journey. With coaching as a major component, it holds the promise and the beauty of the unknown, revealed only through discovery questioning, "egoless-ness," outrageous requesting, truth-saying, and laser informing. Through coaching, you can *consciously* and *intentionally* design the life you want. I encourage you to navigate the road, bridge gaps, and make the shifts that are critical to realizing your dreams.

May your steps be ordered as you step out on faith so that your territory will be expanded. Welcome to *your* amazing journey!

Jylla Moore Foster

PART I

THE CRYSTAL STAIRS
LEADERSHIP JOURNEY

Life for me ain't been no crystal stair . . .
But all the time
I'se been a-climbin' on . . .
FROM "MOTHER TO SON" BY LANGSTON HUGHES
The Collected Poems of Langston Hughes

D r. Mattie Lakin's literature class met in a classroom of the Harriet Tubman Little Theater on the campus of Livingstone College. Standing erect, she recited the masterful, poetic works of Langston Hughes and clearly enunciated each word. Maybe it was the cadence of her contralto voice or the power of the words that seared my consciousness with the message I still carry with me today: *You have to keep climbing, even when "life ain't been no crystal stair."* The plaintive yet profound message of Hughes' poem "Mother to Son" was a reminder that despite my circumstances or the obstacles in my path, I could dictate my future as long as I continued to climb.

If anyone ever wrote the story of my journey, it would contain a series of major shifts and moments in time that shaped the person I have become:

➤ From growing up in the segregated South to experiencing the integration of schools in Salisbury, N.C.;

➤ From studying at the predominantly black Livingstone College as a Samuel E. Duncan scholar to graduating from predominantly white Indiana University as a Consortium for Graduate Study in Business Fellow;

➤ From achieving as a vice president at IBM to being founder, president and CEO of Crystal Stairs, Inc., my life's passion;

➤ From behaving as a dominant, conscientious person to enjoying motherhood with influence and steadiness in life; and

➤ From leading a group of 100,000 women as the international president of Zeta Phi Beta Sorority to honoring the true Source of my power.

Today, I find myself in the midst of an amazing odyssey. The roads I traveled to get here provided lessons at each juncture and helped me climb the next step. The result was the establishment of the Crystal Stairs Leadership Journey and the 12 Leadership Assets™, which are based on my successful corporate experience and what I have learned as the owner of my own leadership coaching, training, and consulting business.

Scores of books have been written about leadership. They analyze it, define it, and refine it. The reason there are so many is that we are learning that the concept of leadership is not finite; it continues to evolve. It is a process. It is a journey. No journey is the same. We seek our own understanding.

So, what makes this book different? The Crystal Stairs Leadership Journey engages a *conscious* and *intentional* effort to help you develop and implement 12 Leadership Assets™ that I have found to be essential to personal growth and professional development. Coupled with a development framework and an action plan, the Crystal Stairs Leadership Journey provides the means to assess objectively where you are in your life and helps you map the course to where you want to be. It's a self-guided journey in which you choose the path you want to travel.

THE 12 LEADERSHIP ASSETS™

The framework developed for the Crystal Stairs Leadership Journey required a tremendous amount of "think time." I needed to identify the skills that were critical to success at each crossroad in my life. After all, I was a student of IBM where "THINK" was a mantra, and I learned it well. With that guiding light, I studied, questioned, researched, and networked until I became comfortable with the 12 Leadership Assets™. My life as a leadership coach incorporates all of these invaluable lessons and skills I acquired during my two decades at IBM and years of community service work.

Recognizing that only I could take responsibility for my personal and professional development, at some point, I began *consciously* and *intentionally* to adapt these competencies to my daily life. Being able to leverage, manage, and utilize these skills helped me thrive, even though I was not fully aware of their power and value. These 12 Leadership Assets™ are the tools I use to succeed as I climb the crystal stairs.

LEADERSHIP ASSETS™			
Coaching			
Attitude and Behavior			
Change		Communication	
Diversity	Performance		Teamwork
Technology	Time Management	Service	Work/Life Equation
Personal and Professional Framework			

COACHING
Harness the Power of Coaching
A professionally trained and certified coach serves as a motivator, consultant, or sounding board for individuals, businesses, or organizations to unleash unlimited potential and achieve goals resulting in lasting change. Harnessing the power of coaching identifies possibilities, positions options, and works through challenges to bridge gaps and effectuate shifts.

ATTITUDE AND BEHAVIOR
Exhibit an Affirmative Attitude and Purposeful Behavior

Attitude (the external reflection of your feelings) and behavior (how you act or respond in any given situation) are two major factors that impact your future, from your ability to progress in your career to your ability to have healthy and happy relationships. When you understand attitude and behavior, you realize you have choices, and the moment you choose to have both an affirmative attitude and purposeful behavior, you determine the course of your future.

CHANGE
Ride the Crests of Change

Change is an inevitability of life. It fosters your growth and development while fueling the sources of energy. The challenge is to "be prepared." Understanding the process of bridging gaps as you end an event, travel through, and start anew is the best approach for welcoming change in your life.

COMMUNICATION
Communicate in a Dynamic, Essential, and Effective Manner

Dynamic communication is two-way communication. It is the clarity of the message as well as the listener's ability to receive it. To be a dynamic communicator, you must also be an effective listener. It is sensitivity to and management of the messenger's chosen format to deliver the message.

DIVERSITY
Prize Diversity

Treasuring everyone, irrespective of race, gender, ethnicity, sexual orientation, age, religion, and/or level of expertise is prizing diversity. It is based on the belief that this dynamic interaction will benefit all participants, as well as the bottom line.

PERFORMANCE
Excel in Performance

To excel in performance, you need a plan that covers every facet of your life; it means self-ownership of your own power to determine your destiny. It is both qualitative and quantitative and measures your accomplishments and charts your progress as you achieve success. It is an essential component of the journey.

TEAMWORK
Exercise Your Teamwork
Break out of the mold of individualism and "me-ism" and share your expertise to resolve a challenge or accomplish a task. Leveraging a pool of talents and resources creates value for everyone. Know your role and how best to flex to serve the interests of the whole. Develop your personal and professional team.

TECHNOLOGY
Surf the Waves of Technology
The integral role that technology plays in your life and your work mandates understanding how to utilize it both as an information provider and productivity tool. The demands of new generations are rapidly dictating the quick pace of change in the world of technology. Those interactions are providing access and choices as never before experienced in history.

TIME MANAGEMENT
Command Your Time Management
One of the greatest skills of a *conscious* and *intentional* leader is the ability to govern the use of time. Time governance is self-management, the acquiring and implementation of good habits, priority setting, and sensitivity to others' time expectations.

SERVICE
Eternalize a Life of Service
Service is the act of giving of yourself, your time, and your expertise to create value in your community and in the lives of others. It is a means of creating your legacy by giving back from your heart.

WORK/LIFE EQUATION
Calibrate Your Work/Life Equation
The energy that we exert on our work plan and our life plan is an equation that sometimes changes based on shifts in priorities. At any given moment, you have to choose the weight of the numerator and

denominator that make up that equation by determining what's *most* important. It means setting priorities while being flexible in order to work your plan.

PERSONAL AND PROFESSIONAL FRAMEWORK
Crystallize Your Personal and Professional Framework
Uncertainty about who you are and what you believe will result in a life buffeted by winds like a kite on a string. Established personal and professional principles become your life's framework and prevent you from unconsciously compromising your values. Maintaining a profile of the major guidelines that frame your life is as important as maintaining a professional file.

BECOMING CONSCIOUS AND INTENTIONAL

My life experiences have taught me that we have the power to take control of our destiny. It means more than managing the unique talents and abilities with which you have been blessed. You have the ability to create *consciously* and *intentionally* the type of life you want to lead.

You cannot be successful when you set vague, idealistic goals without a specific target in mind. A *conscious* and *intentional* life is based on insight, intuition, dialectical (analytical and critical) thinking, and the determination to affirm honesty, fairness, integrity, decisiveness, dedication, passion, and planning.

THE CONSCIOUS/INTENTIONAL BAROMETER©

If you want to create value with your life and achieve your objectives, you have to be *conscious* of what it is you want and *intentional* about making it happen. You have to make clear choices, as well as clear distinctions.

	CONSCIOUS	UNCONSCIOUS
INTENTIONAL	*Conscious/Intentional (CI)* Aware of everything around you and your ability to influence your environment through informed choices that you make	*Unconscious/ Intentional(UI)* Unaware, but making choices based on what seems right at the moment
UNINTENTIONAL	*Conscious/ Unintentional(CU)* Aware but not exercising choice	*Unconscious/ Unintentional(UU)* Go with the flow. . . No clue

In your daily routine, what type of life are you leading? Based on the definitions above, put a check in the appropriate category:

#	ACTIVITY	CI	UI	CU	UU
1	Waking up with passion and focusing on your day ahead				
2	Morning prayer or meditation				
3	Taking a shower and dressing				
4	Drinking coffee/tea/juice				
5	First of eight glasses of water				
6	Eating breakfast				
7	Morning conversations with spouse/significant others				
8	Reading the morning paper				
9	Watching the morning news on television				
10	Driving to work				
11	Taking the bus/train to work				
12	Parking your car and walking to your office building				
13	Walking from the bus stop/train station to your office building				
14	Riding the elevator or walking up the steps to your office				
15	Your interaction with co-workers				
16	Your interaction with the administrative assistants				
17	Planning your work day				
18	Tackling the pile of work on your desk				

continued . . .

#	ACTIVITY	CI	UI	CU	UU
19	Voice mail				
20	Email				
21	First telephone conversations				
22	Morning business meetings				
23	Conversations with your managers				
24	Conversations with your peers				
25	Conversations with your employees				
26	Coffee break				
27	Elevator conversations				
28	Lunch-line conversations				
29	Choosing your lunch				
30	Eating your lunch				
31	Afternoon business meetings				
32	Afternoon coffee break				
33	Voice mail (second, third, or "x" time)				
34	Email (second, third, or "x" time)				
35	Finishing afternoon projects				
36	Planning the next day's work				
37	Working late				
38	Leaving the office				
39	Interactions with manager, co-workers, and/or staff				
40	Walking from the office to the parking lot				
41	Walking from the office to the bus/train station				
42	Driving/riding home				
43	Cell phone conversations				
44	Evening conversations with spouse or significant others				
45	Evening conversation with children or friends				
46	Watching television				
47	Exercise				
48	Undressing for bed				
49	Evening prayer or meditation				
50	Going to sleep with the awareness that you've had a worthwhile and productive day				
	TOTALS				

Add up the total in each of the four categories. In which category do you have the most checkmarks? If it is not in the *conscious* and *intentional* category, imagine how much you are missing as part of your daily routine. How might your life change if all of your activities were listed in the upper left-hand corner of the matrix? Can you make *conscious* and *intentional* choices about how you use your time and live your life?

THE LEADERSHIP ASSETS™ DEVELOPMENT FRAMEWORK©

The Leadership Assets™ Development Framework© (illustrated on the next page) will help you move from life in the unconscious/unintentional zone to being present in every moment of every day. It consists of four major actions: Learn, Assess and Reflect, Plan, and Execute. Each component is explained below.

Learn

Due North! is the compass for *learning*. To learn means to discover. This book offers opportunities to explore new terrain, seek answers, and choose new directions based on what you discover as a result of your involved study. Record "your story" as you attend seminars, training programs, and meetings. Try to log the learning into an asset. Find opportunities to update your skills and foundation on a frequent basis.

Assess and Reflect

An action plan document is provided at the end of each chapter. It challenges you to *assess* where you are and *reflect* on where you want to go. From helping you summarize the lessons you learned to creating a checklist of steps you want to take, the plan provides a consistent way for pinpointing, recording, and focusing on areas that can be strengthened. As you complete each chapter and document what you've learned, the plan becomes a synopsis of where you are in your journey to master the asset. Once you've completed your study of all twelve assets, you'll consolidate them into a summary assessment.

THE LEADERSHIP ASSETS™ DEVELOPMENT FRAMEWORK©

PERSONAL TRANSFORMATION

STRUCTURED LEARNING MODULES

ASSESS/REFLECT
- ☐ CS Leadership Journey Assessment©
- ☐ Assessments Profile Record
- ☐ 360° Feedback Assessment
- ☐ CS Technology Checklist©
- ☐ Conscious/Intentional Barometer©
- ☐ CS Personal/Professional Framework (PPF)©

LEARN
- ☐ Due North!
- ☐ Leadership Assets™ Action Plan©
- ☐ "Your Story"

LEADERSHIP ASSETS™		
Coaching		
Attitude and Behavior		
Change	Communication	
	Performance	Teamwork
Diversity	Time Management	Service	Work/Life Equation
Technology		
Personal and Professional Framework		

PLAN
- ☐ CS Performance Plan©
- ☐ CS Development Plan©
- ☐ CS Life Compass (LC)©
- ☐ CS Strategic Life Plan Framework (LPF)©

EXECUTE
- ☐ Coach
- ☐ CS Network Group
- ☐ Teleclasses
- ☐ Seminars
- ☐ CS Leadership Institute

DYNAMIC, SITUATIONAL INTERACTION

PROFESSIONAL DEVELOPMENT

© Crystal Stairs, Inc., 2002
Note: CS = Crystal Stairs

Plan

Assessments are the maps that guide you along your journey. They provide an objective analysis and establish a foundation from which you can grow. They highlight indicators for the action steps needed to begin living and working in a *conscious* and *intentional* manner. There are many different approaches and assessments available, as well as programs that can be customized to provide you with greater awareness. What's important to note is that they reveal information for a plan of action to be developed.

When completing an assessment, you will not be competing against someone else for a higher score. Assessments are not tests. Sharing behavior styles, strengths, and growth areas with someone does not necessarily mean you need to mirror the same steps. The assessments evaluate you as an individual, and your course of action is developed according to your needs.

Based on what you discover developing your action plans, the Crystal Stairs Leadership Assets™ Journey Assessment, which can be found in Appendix A, will help you create a lifelong learning and planning process that outlines specific steps required to achieve your objectives. Using this assessment, you will be able to set priorities, choose a point of focus, and develop a month-to-month action plan. The assessment also provides you with the flexibility to revise the plan whenever you make a new discovery or want to change your focus.

Execute

Once you have a plan, it's important that its *execution* be divided into phases based on priorities and needs. A coach can help with execution by monitoring a critical element along your journey—FOCUS! The constant discussions to facilitate positive shifts will steer your plan in the right direction. Making verbal commitments that remain at the forefront of your life generates steady, consistent progress and achievements.

THE THOUSAND-MILE JOURNEY

An old saying reminds us that a thousand-mile journey begins with a single step. The Crystal Stairs Leadership Journey is the first step on your quest to have an ordered—rather than managed—Work/Life

Equation. Since I began employing these assets in my life, I have experienced renewed determination about my work and clarity about who I am and what's important to me. At the same time, I have found a way to live a life of service that creates value for other people. Being a leadership coach, trainer, speaker, and consultant is my passion and my mission.

Now that you've taken the first step, welcome to the journey!

PART II

12 LEADERSHIP ASSETS™

1. Harness the Power of COACHING
2. Exhibit an Affirmative ATTITUDE AND Purposeful BEHAVIOR
3. Ride the Crests of CHANGE
4. COMMUNICATE in a Dynamic, Essential, and Effective Manner
5. Prize DIVERSITY
6. Excel in PERFORMANCE
7. Exercise Your TEAMWORK
8. Surf the Waves of TECHNOLOGY
9. Command Your TIME MANAGEMENT
10. Eternalize a Life of SERVICE
11. Calibrate Your WORK/LIFE EQUATION
12. Crystallize Your PERSONAL AND PROFESSIONAL FRAMEWORK

A professionally trained and certified coach serves as a motivator, consultant, or sounding board for individuals, businesses, or organizations to unleash unlimited potential and achieve goals resulting in lasting change. Harnessing the power of coaching identifies possibilities, positions options, and works through challenges to bridge gaps and effectuate shifts.

COACHING

To live a life without regret, what will be your choices and what do you want the results to be?

AUDRA BOHANNON
Senior Vice President, J. Howard & Associates, Inc.

Some say coaching is the "art" of the question. When was the last time you painted a masterpiece?

BRYAN DUROCHER
Success Coach, Durocher Enterprises

What would you dare to dream if you knew it would come true?

JOVITA JENKINS
Executive Coach, Ajides International, Inc.

What would it take to schedule time with yourself, for one hour, three times per week, to accomplish something that you really wanted that you've kept on the back burner?

BARBARA McDUFFIE KAHLER
President, Leadership In Action, LLC

What is the most significant change you've made in your life? What assets did you use to successfully maneuver the change?

JACKIE NAGEL
President, Synnovatia

oaching begins with questions that require reflection, forward thinking, and bridging gaps. So it is appropriate that I share questions that will hopefully cause you to think about the Coach Approach of discovery and learning.

When I joined IBM, it was not uncommon for corporations to pay for MBA degrees and, in some cases, Ph.Ds. They also offered skills-building workshops, career counseling services, internal and external placement information, and company-sponsored workshops or classes to help improve performance. But with technological advances leading to enhanced productivity and the emergence of "e-learning" options, and with competition forcing corporations constantly to shrink the bottom line, the days of unlimited training, corporate scholarships, engraved gold watches, and retirement with full-salary pensions have become dreams of the past.

As organizational structures become more complex, the need to know how to navigate through them is becoming more intense. How do we remain flexible and fluid in an environment in which the paradigm is constantly shifting? How do we manage when external forces contribute heavily to the internal transformations that are required to remain a viable competitor? The answer is the Coach Approach.

We've all experienced different types of coaches in our lives: parents, teachers, religious or spiritual leaders, bankers, financial planners, personal fitness trainers, or insurance agents. But to focus the direction of your business or organization, pinpoint the direction of your team, and enhance your professional development or personal growth, a coach, either internal or external, provides the bridge over troubled waters.

WHAT IS COACHING?

A professionally trained and certified coach can serve as a facilitator, motivator, consultant, or sounding board to help a business, an organization, or individuals unleash unlimited potential and achieve goals that will bring about lasting change. A coach maximizes people, performance, productivity, and profitability. But unlike a coach in sports, who gives the team a playbook and adjusts the strategy as the game progresses, a leadership coach helps the client determine what steps are needed (the client writes the playbook) to achieve outlined goals and then provides support and feedback from the sidelines as the game plan is implemented. A coach doesn't flinch if the ball is dropped. The goal is to create a safe haven. A coach shines a laser beam on blind spots and targets focused truths. The coach provides feedback to *awaken* clients to the gaps in their business processes, organizations, or their lives and helps them build the bridge.

Unlike psychotherapy, which dissects one's present life by analyzing personal history, coaching focuses on the present. It shapes the future by shifting the context in which decisions are made. How is this done?

DISCOVERING WHERE YOU NEED TO GROW

One of the most important tools coaches use is assessments. "To know where you need to go," a wise person once said, "you must know where you've been." Throughout this book, I reference assessments. There are various types of assessments. They analyze behavior, personality, values, interpersonal relationship skills, working with teams, understanding diversity, handling change, managing your time, and several other skills. Assessments identify the areas in your life where you might be stuck or weak, or they might pinpoint specific skills that you may want to develop. Most critical is that assessments provide a nonjudgmental and objective tool for self-inspection and self-reflection. They become a foundation for the journey and create the means for you to develop *conscious* and *intentional* mile-markers for the path. Refer to Appendix B for a summary of recommended assessments you can complete to strengthen your understanding of yourself and others.

THE LANGUAGE OF COACHING

Coaching has its own tools, language, and requisite set of skills. The language will be applied as we travel our leadership journey.

> *Coach Approach*
> The use of specific communication techniques that result in dramatic shifts. By skillfully responding to the dynamics of the encounter, a coach provides a pathway to greater understanding.

Coachable Moments
The point in time when the coach creates the environment in which an individual is open to taking in new information that will affect a shift in his/her knowledge and behavior.

Inside Out Shifts
Those internal shifts in thinking, attitude, or position that, when manifested outwardly, result in an observable behavior change.

Contextual Listening
Coaches are trained, through listening, to understand an individual's frame of reference, his/her wants, needs, and concerns, or what is not said.

Discovery Questioning
The process of using provocative or sharply focused questions to help individuals discover their truth.

Laser Informing
Delivery of a truthful message that is timely, personal, relevant, and succinct.

Gap Bridging
The place between where you are presently and where you want to be. Gap bridging helps clarify the desired outcomes and creates the structural plan of action.

The Coaching Conversation
Using five basic steps to facilitate a coaching session.
➢ Focus the conversation
➢ Discover possibilities
➢ Make an action plan
➢ Remove the barriers
➢ Review and formulate next steps

Truth-Saying
The coach is expected to tell the truth, something businesses and individuals are not always accustomed to hearing.

Outrageous Requesting
Coaches ask more of their clients than the clients ask of themselves; this forces them to stretch their thinking of possibilities.

Celebrating "What Is"
The coach's goal is to help a person shift from the attitude that "Life is a struggle" to the belief that "Life is a challenge, with endless possibilities," worthy of applause.

Tolerations
Habits or actions based on a false sense of responsibility or unrealistic expectations.

Extreme Self-Care
Establishing personal time and taking care of yourself is an element critical to success. Extreme self-care is a necessity.

A skilled coach is a committed listener who, during sessions, exhibits single-minded focus on the client's goals. Tracy Stevens, an instructor at Corporate Coach University International (CCUI), characterizes this skill as being able to "listen to the point of disappearing." That thought helped me reframe my understanding of contextual listening and my ability to deliver a pertinent response. Using "discovery questioning" to pinpoint concerns, options, and potential opportunities, the coach helps the client focus on specific action areas.

The coach also helps clients eliminate roadblocks along with artificial or real barriers in executing their plan. Periodically probing and encouraging, the coach helps keep the client focused and moving in the direction of achieving goals and objectives. From being an avid, contextual listener to utilizing intuition, the coach's goal is to be ego-less and agenda-less, immersing himself or herself in the client's needs for a specified period of time. The skilled coach can, for example, zero in on a negative attitude and facilitate the client's shift to a positive outlook.

Just as important, the coach can help eliminate tolerations. By helping you set aside time on your calendar to ensure your positive, total well-being, a coach directs you away from focusing only on the needs of others and toward making extreme self-care an integral part of your routine.

The coach can facilitate a coachable moment in the client's life that causes a shift resulting in a measure of success. In the coachable moment, the coach creates the environment in which the client is open to taking in the information affecting the shift in knowledge *and* behavior. It is the coach's job to listen for and seize those moments so that the change is both beneficial and permanent. Coaches strive to "be" the coach instead of "doing the job" of coaching.

How do you want to be coached? This is an important discussion to have with your coach. The chart on the following page, used with permission of CoachWorks International, provides a communication framework to steer the discussion.

COACH versus MENTOR, MANAGER, LEADER

As a former IBM manager, leader, and executive, I mentored a number of individuals inside the corporation and in other corporations. I mentored them either to achieve a skill or to establish relationships that would be beneficial to their careers. I mentored organizational leaders who wanted to strengthen their leadership skills or shift the direction of their groups. In a mentoring relationship, the mentee has full responsibility for taking suggested actions to advance the agenda that the pair has set to facilitate advancement and growth.

As a manager, it was my responsibility to champion the agenda of the company, measure results against targets, and inspire and motivate teams to achieve those targets. I had deliverables to produce and messages to communicate. Often, I saluted the flag and moved forward. I was trained to manage. I developed my unique management "style." My "D" and "C" behaviors (see Chapter 2 on Attitude and Behavior) were visible and often demonstrated.

As a leader, I thrived on creating and shaping new possibilities. I worked with others to establish the vision, and together we proceeded to accomplish the mission, goals, objectives, and tasks. I built supportive teams and kept my eyes focused on the end game.

As a coach, I focus solely on the client's agenda.

THE COACHING CHECKLIST©

How do you want to be coached?

Name: _____ Date: _____

Use the checklist below to identify those preferences you have about how you want to work with your Coach. Place a check mark in all the boxes that apply.

Structure of the Process
❏ Free flow of ideas
❏ Brainstorming with focus
❏ Some structure
❏ Lots of structure
❏ Other: _____

Pace
❏ Fast pace
❏ Moderate pace
❏ Slow pace
❏ No predetermined pace
❏ Other: _____

Listening & Understanding
❏ Listen and paraphrase
❏ Listen & ask questions
❏ Listen and probe
❏ Interrupt when needed
❏ Other: _____

When Making Decisions
❏ Want to make them quickly
❏ Want to make sound ones
❏ Want help exploring options
❏ Want time to consider options
❏ Other: _____

Delivering Information
❏ Give me bottom line
❏ Big picture with info
❏ Need both sides of issue
❏ Need lots of detail first
❏ Other: _____

Relationship
❏ Build rapport quickly
❏ Like to know you're interested

❏ Take time to trust you
❏ Don't trust easily
❏ Other: _____

Confidentiality
❏ Information with me only
❏ Share with appropriate resources
❏ Collaborate with my manager
❏ Collaborate with designees
❏ Other: _____

In Teams
❏ Coach toward leadership
❏ Coach to be a team player
❏ Coach to input my ideas
❏ Coach to look at bigger picture
❏ Other: _____

Acknowledgment
❏ Not very important
❏ For my abilities
❏ For my progress
❏ For the person I am
❏ Other: _____

Integrity
❏ Absolute honesty
❏ Want to see you "walk the talk"
❏ Hold me to my commitments
❏ Need to know guiding principles
❏ Other: _____

Focus of Issues
❏ Business only
❏ Professional development
❏ Professional and personal
❏ Personal
❏ Other: _____

Goals
❏ Like to work toward goals
❏ Change goals as needed
❏ Goals for sessions only
❏ No goals
❏ Other: _____

Projects
❏ Coach me to delegate
❏ Coach to stay focused
❏ Coach to avoid perfection
❏ Other: _____

Calling Me on Things
❏ Be deliberate/ straightforward
❏ Give info and options
❏ Deliver respectfully
❏ Tell me what and build case
❏ Other: _____

Celebrating Accomplishments
❏ Don't make a big deal
❏ Sounds fun, a "must do"
❏ Coach me to celebrate myself
❏ Teach me what it is to do so
❏ Other: _____

Source: © Coachworks International™

CRITICAL DISTINCTIONS

When you look at the roles of the various people in your life, you can establish realistic expectations for the profession of coaching. The coach helps navigate the client to reach goals and to create or facilitate shifts. Coaching requires training on how to use language with as much specificity as that used by a doctor; when completing a prescription, he or she uses language that only a pharmacist can decipher. The language of coaching is as powerful as the interpretation of literary works or an artist's masterpiece.

As a coach focused on the Crystal Stairs Leadership Assets™, I constantly struggle with the degree to which I share my personal experiences when helping to develop solutions for a problem. During each session, my old paradigms are challenged based on new possibilities as business models continue to change in the world. The personal challenge for me, and for any coach, is knowing how close to get to the gray line, remaining ego-less, so as not to prevent the client from discovering his/her own truths or possibilities.

The coach is a professional who thrives on client transformation!

TYPES OF COACHES

As the coaching profession develops, I support the specialties that are emerging. Just as teachers specialize in subjects that drive their passions and thus become experts in their fields of learning, so it is also true with coaches. The varieties are endless and include executive coach, business coach, life coach, health coach, motivational coach, and spirit and soul coach. Expert coaches know their strengths and accentuate them to achieve maximum results with their clients.

To that end, my greatest passion is to work with people who want to make a serious effort to achieve success through personal focus and by learning to engage the 12 Leadership Assets™. I work with businesses that want to develop extraordinary talent on their teams. I define businesses as any person or group that has clients or stakeholders. Therefore, my potential clients include universities, community organizations, small businesses and Fortune 500 corporations. I am a leadership coach.

ENGAGE THE PROCESS

CoachWorks International has developed an excellent "Coaching Model." It summarizes the process and the deliverables. Use this model as you select a coach and as you navigate your journey.

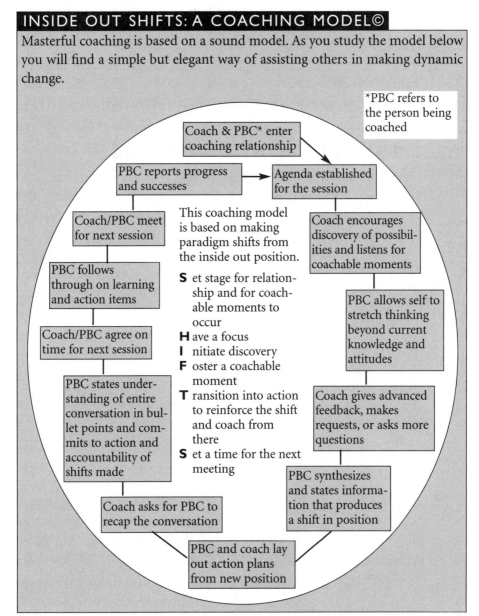

INSIDE OUT SHIFTS: A COACHING MODEL©

Masterful coaching is based on a sound model. As you study the model below you will find a simple but elegant way of assisting others in making dynamic change.

*PBC refers to the person being coached

Coach & PBC* enter coaching relationship

PBC reports progress and successes → Agenda established for the session

Coach/PBC meet for next session

This coaching model is based on making paradigm shifts from the inside out position.

Coach encourages discovery of possibilities and listens for coachable moments

S et stage for relationship and for coachable moments to occur
H ave a focus
I nitiate discovery
F oster a coachable moment
T ransition into action to reinforce the shift and coach from there
S et a time for the next meeting

PBC follows through on learning and action items

Coach/PBC agree on time for next session

PBC allows self to stretch thinking beyond current knowledge and attitudes

Coach gives advanced feedback, makes requests, or asks more questions

PBC states understanding of entire conversation in bullet points and commits to action and accountability of shifts made

PBC synthesizes and states information that produces a shift in position

Coach asks for PBC to recap the conversation

PBC and coach lay out action plans from new position

Source: © CoachWorks International™

It is important to understand when you are ready to engage in the process of coaching. A good coach will assess whether you are "coachable," and will ask you to follow very specific guidelines and often to complete assignments. Coaching is an investment that can pay dramatic dividends, especially if it is done correctly. Seek to engage in the process or develop your own coaching skills to supplement your management style or your leadership approach. These skills are helpful in dealing with your professional work and personal life.

Now that you have been exposed and understand the coaching discipline, it is time to start the work. Contact a coach and take action, using the Coaching Action Plan© on the following page.

THE FINAL THOUGHT . . . COACHING

There are many ways you can add coaching as an asset to your tool kit. Understand it, engage it, do it, be it. Coaching is a tool that can help you execute the plan you derive from your journey. I hope you will participate in what will be a nonstop, amazing adventure.

Harness the Power of Coaching!

COACHING ACTION PLAN©

Client: _____ *Objective:* _____

PRIORITIES	TACTICS	STRATEGIC PLAYS	MILESTONES	MEASURES	S T A T U S
What needs to be done?	How will you do it?	What are long-term considerations?	When will it be done?	How will you know it's successful?	
1.					
2.					
3.					

NUGGETS
1.
2.
3.

ASSESSMENT: (How well achieved measures)

© *Crystal Stairs, Inc. 2002*

COACHING

LESSONS LEARNED (NUGGETS)

1 _____
2 _____
3 _____

CHECKLIST

- ☐ 1 Focuses on priorities and goals
- ☐ 2 Identifies and bridges gaps
- ☐ 3 Comfortable with accepting and delivering truths
- ☐ 4 Executes the coaching model
- ☐ 5 Asks laser questions
- ☐ 6 Makes clear distinctions
- ☐ 7 Listens and responds to contextual meaning
- ☐ 8 Challenges and achieves outrageous requests
- ☐ 9 Effectively engages a coach
- ☐ 10 Lives intentionally
- ☐ 11 Consciously plans extreme self-care
- ☐ 12 Celebrates "what is"
- ___ *Total*

ACTIONS PLANNED　　　　COMPLETION DATE

1 _____　　_____
2 _____　　_____
3 _____　　_____
4 _____　　_____
5 _____　　_____

BARRIERS/BLIND SPOTS

1 _____
2 _____
3 _____

ACHIEVEMENTS

1 _____
2 _____
3 _____

2. EXHIBIT AN AFFIRMATIVE ATTITUDE AND PURPOSEFUL BEHAVIOR

Attitude (the external reflection of your feelings) and behavior (how you act or respond in any given situation) are two major factors that impact your future, from your ability to progress in your career to your ability to have healthy and happy relationships. When you understand attitude and behavior, you realize you have choices, and the moment you choose to have both an affirmative attitude and purposeful behavior, you determine the course of your future.

ATTITUDE AND BEHAVIOR

The best thing about your attitude is that if it's bad, it can be made better, and if it's good, it can be made even greater.

KEITH HARRELL
Motivational Speaker and Author

Don't ask, "What is it about them that rubs me wrong?"
Ask, "What is it about me that makes what they do rub me wrong?"

BOB PICHA
PsychoGraphics, Inc.

Many of us have preconceived notions about everything imaginable. We can't help it. We learn them from our families, friends, in school, and from our religious institutions. When we get a foot on the corporate ladder, we bring those preconceptions with us. We already have decided how much work we're *supposed* to do; how much money we're *supposed* to make; how many windows there are *supposed* to be in our office (or cubicle); how our managers, coworkers, or subordinates are *supposed* to address us, respond to us, treat us.

27

If things don't work out the way we think they should, we go *there*: We flash *attitude problem* like the neon in Times Square. We don't realize that, unlike Times Square, people are repelled rather than attracted to the lights. Talk about stopping a career that's on the fast track! An *attitude problem* can derail the whole train.

YOUR ATTITUDE IS YOUR CHOICE

What impact has your attitude had on your career? Your personal life? What changes do you think you need to make?

Attitude is a choice. At any given moment, you can choose to be positive, negative, or indifferent. But every choice has a consequence. When you focus on the positive, your life moves forward. If you choose indifference, life will be at a momentary standstill. But because nothing stands still for long, life will begin to slip backward. Negativity is draining, depressing, and oppressive. It makes us feel confused and misunderstood. It makes us withdraw, retreat, and clam up in fear, doubt, and self-recrimination. When we're dealing with our *attitude problem*, no one suffers as much as we do ourselves.

Unless you consciously spend time sorting through your attitude or approach and reevaluate your perspective while soaring above the dark clouds, you, too, will become an *attitude problem*. Assessing your attitude-related issues can serve as a compass to help you find the path out of the forest. It will help you understand how a simple thing such as your attitude can affect things as complex as the goals of your corporation, your organization, your family, your future.

Keith Harrell was featured in a *Wall Street Journal* article entitled "The Selling of a Golden Speech: On the Motivational Circuit, a Star with Attitude." It noted the positive effect he was having with his motivational message: "Attitude Is Everything." Keith believes that "The most valuable asset you can possess is a *positive attitude toward your life*." I've heard him deliver his message on several occasions, and each time it's a blessing.

Complete the following attitude assessment developed by Keith Harrell and contained in his book *Attitude Is Everything*.

ATTITUDE ASSESSMENT©

On a sheet of paper, make a list of the negative attitudes that may have held you back in the past. Beside each one, write down what you think the source of that attitude might be. What is the baggage and what does it contain? What past experiences? What hurt? What shame? What anger? What jealousy?

This can be a painful and emotional exercise, so I advise you to go off by yourself somewhere or to ask someone who knows you well to help. A brother, sister, spouse, or parent might have clues that you can't see. This is a cleansing experience. Sometimes you have to scrape hard, so don't be afraid. And don't run from what you find. It's part of who you are. There's no shame in it. What's past is past. Root it out, recognize it, respect it. It's a part of your life; deal with it.

1. How do you respond to stressful situations?

This is where a bad attitude can quickly rise to the surface. When you are pressured to get something done, to perform at a higher level, or to meet high expectations, do you:

a. Get angry?
b. Become depressed?
c. Throw up your arms in despair?
d. Get energized?

Examine which of these responses is most similar to yours when you become stressed out. Then look at why you respond in that manner. What attitude drives you to respond in that way?

2. Do you tend to look at the world in a pessimistic way?

Pessimism is the outward expression of a bad attitude. If you seem always to find the downside of an otherwise great situation, if you look for the dark lining in the silver clouds, if you see the glass as half-empty rather than half-full, you too may be suffering from bad-attitude-induced pessimism. It is not fun being a pessimist and pessimists aren't much fun to be around. They are dream-killers. Their dreams and the dreams of people around them get shot down.

© *Harrell Performance Systems, Inc. 2000*

Based on the results of your assessment, you can create a plan of action and a set of goals to develop the attitude asset. The plan would incorporate your vision of your future and honestly assess what changes you will have to make in order to achieve your goal.

ATTITUDE AND VALUES

Bill J. Bonnstetter, founder and president of Target Training International (TTI), is the author of the book *If I Knew Then What I Know Now*. It provides insight into attitudes and values. TTI's Personal Interests, Attitudes and Values™ (PIAV) Assessment, based on work by Eduard Spranger in his book *Types of Men* (1928), categorizes attitudes toward and values about life in six ways:

> *Theoretical:* Seeks knowledge, understanding, and "truth." Learns by reading, watching, and doing. Asks many questions.

> *Utilitarian:* Applies resources to solve problems. Hates wasting time. Will work long hours for gain. Always wants Return On Investment (ROI).

> *Aesthetic:* Must have harmony in their world, from surroundings to relationships with others. Intuitive and instinctive.

> *Social:* Deep concern for the welfare of others because it is the "right thing to do." Helps others.

> *Individualist:* Controls self and others. Wants to advance and achieve. Uses power to accomplish goals. Visionary.

> *Traditional:* Lives by the "rule book" and believes in tradition. Holds others accountable. Judgmental.

While the summary merely scratches the surface, it would be extremely beneficial to explore your attitudes and values by taking this assessment as noted in Appendix B.

MY "ATTITUDE" STORY

I wanted to be a vice president at IBM. To make that aspiration a reality, I constantly reflected on the type of attitude I needed. I had to believe that I had the professional talent, expertise, and skills to be successful, even if there were people in my environment—myself included —telling me something different.

With each promotion at IBM, I had to withstand the external and internal whispers. Those voices would test my resolve and confidence and challenge my belief in my professional abilities. During those times, I often thought about the attitude of great athletes. Whenever football or baseball players step on the field or whenever basketball players begin their shoot-arounds, they *consciously* and *intentionally* focus on winning. They continue to envision a positive outcome until the final buzzer or the third out in the bottom of the ninth inning. Even if they lose the game, they usually don't spend time dwelling on the loss. Instead, they begin to focus on the strategy for the next game and plan how they will play differently the next time. They begin to envision their next victory. It wasn't easy, and it didn't happen overnight, but I began to understand the link between attitude and success.

Another tool I have used to *adjust my attitude* was having a confidante at work. This person was neither a manager nor a mentor. The discussion simply allowed me to have an open and honest dialogue. I called them "truth-telling sessions."

"Do you think I have an attitude problem about this issue?" I would candidly ask. My confidante would tell me the truth. Even if I didn't always like the answer, this person helped me see the bigger picture. My attitude was no longer an obstacle. Rather, it became the tool I used to take the steps necessary for my professional and personal growth.

COACHABLE MOMENTS

There are other, less-obvious, attitude-related situations. Suppose you are assigned a new manager. Maybe you've heard negative things about the person from other employees. Maybe you were in line for the job, and the new manager got it instead. What do you do when co-workers criticize the new manager or when your internal negative voice speaks loudly? What do you do the first time your new manager gives you an assignment and your negative voice yells (because it wants to make sure you get *this* point): "Who does she think she is? I know more about this job than she *ever* will. I'm not going to do a thing she tells me?" With your headlights flashing *attitude problem* in day-glow orange, what do you think will happen to your relationship with your new manager? What impact will that have on your job? Are you hearing the screeching brakes on the fast track again?

The great thing about *consciously* and *intentionally* working on your attitude is that turning the key that opens the door to success begins with a *choice.* No one can make us feel anything we don't *want* to feel. The moment I made the decision to soar above the forest, the moment I decided I would do my best in every job to which I was promoted, the sun began to shine. I realized how important it was to be able to self-reflect about my attitude, to dissect it and recognize the triggers that caused me to respond one way or another. Exercising choice about your attitude is a critical and necessary skill. And just like any other skill needed for professional advancement, it requires *assessment* and *training.*

THE COACH APPROACH

A coach will tell you the truth (truth-saying) about your attitude and help you develop a plan of action for change. Coaching helps you to discover the possibilities that already exist within your life, rather than just focus on the problems.

If you don't have a confidante who will deliver tough messages with laser focus, then a coach can fill the void. With no agenda and no ego, the coach creates an environment for exploring the depth of the issues. "Don't ask me the question," I often say, "if you don't want to hear the answer." A coach will ask you the questions that bring your answers to the surface of reality: right between the eyes.

Working on your attitude, however, is just half of the equation. Your attitude affects behavior. Even if you *think* you have made *conscious* and *intentional* changes in your attitude, what is your behavior saying about you?

YOUR BEHAVIOR IS WHAT OTHER PEOPLE SEE

Behavior is how you respond to situations within a given environment with a perceived degree of control. Successful people *consciously* and *intentionally* plan their behavior by making a *conscious* and *intentional* decision to understand themselves, as well as others. That *conscious* understanding of the behavior style of the people in your environment, and knowing yourself, equips you with the tools you need to be flexible and successful in any given situation.

The following chart provides a graphic of behavior styles. It also incorporates words that youth might use to describe behavior as depicted in Inscape Publishing's I-Sight® Behavior Assessment.

DISC® BUTTERFLY CHART

DOMINANCE		INFLUENCE	
Power	Action	Popularity	Groups
Authority	Results	Recognition	Impressions
Prestige	Challenges	Freedom of	Optimistic
D		expression **i**	
In-charge	Direct	Persuading	Interested
Deciding	Active	Enthusiastic	Lively
CONSCIENTIOUSNESS		STEADINESS	
Defined	Details	Status Quo	Predictable
expectations	Standard	Routine	Patience
Accurate	Systematic	Credit	Skilled
Quality			
"Why?" **C**		**S**	
Careful	Concerned	Supportive	Easy-going
Quiet	Correct	Friendly	Cooperative

© *Crystal Stairs, Inc. 2002*

People who exhibit *D-Dominance* behavior often want immediate answers because they need to make quick decisions. People who are *C-Conscientiousness* are detail-oriented, always weighing pros and cons and wanting to know the facts. The person whose style is *I-Influence* is a popular, people-oriented person who has a history of motivating the team. The *S-Steadiness* person is noted for consistent behavior, unending patience, and loyalty.

Often, an employee's or manager's style is misinterpreted in terms of competence or personality issues. If this style is different from ours, we call our co-workers "empty-suiters," "control freaks," "techies," or use other descriptors.

An example of behavior in action is team dynamics. By dissecting and understanding behavior, you can help your team members contribute to the work effort based on the individual behaviors they manifest in a given situation. Every team needs someone who will take the reigns (D) of control. Every team needs someone who is interested in the needs of the team members (I) and who will celebrate their successes. Every team needs someone who is easygoing and focused (S), as well as someone who understands that the devil is in the details (C). When each team member's behavior style is understood and you, as the leader, fill in the gaps, the entire work effort is maximized to achieve peak performance.

Flexibility is the *conscious* and *intentional* evaluation of any given situation or environment. It is understanding what is missing and adjusting your behavior—and encouraging the adjustment of others—to meet the needs of the entire team. You may now be wondering if being flexible is analogous to acquiescing or suppressing your behavior for the sake of others. In corporate environments, like it or not, there are expectations. There are leaders and followers, and we're expected to know our respective roles. We also are expected to control, manage, and facilitate. At any given time, understanding the role you need to play and the behavior you need to exhibit is crucial to the course of your career.

If, for example, you are the lead executive on a project with the responsibility for its success, isn't it important that you know your team's behavior styles when delegating the roles and tasks? Think about some of the people with whom you work. Think about environments in which you work with groups of people, business teams, case-study groups, church organizations, or even student-government leadership teams. In most instances you will find that *dominance* people dictate the answers. People whose behavior style is *influence* will seek consensus. *Steady* people will wait until they are asked before they will tell you what they think. *Conscientiousness* people need detail, detail, and more detail. Specific behavior plays out in most environments, but you can flex and control your behavior as the situation dictates. It is important that you know your team members' behavior style as well as your own. The DiSC® behavior assessment is an indispensable tool for navigation on your journey.

Natalie Van Der Pump expressed the value of the DiSC® assessment best when she shared with me, "Awareness is awesome, and I want to own some of the stuff that was in the report that I know to be true!"

MY "BEHAVIOR" STORY

My DiSC® assessment indicated that my behavior preference was a high *DC—dominance and conscientiousness.* I do tend to be very focused, in charge, and detail-oriented. I have to stretch to deal with people whose behavior style is *influence* or *steadiness.* Thankfully, I had a secretary at IBM who helped me recognize the value of working with different behavior styles.

Susie Wylie worked with me when I was IBM's channels executive, based in Cincinnati. She was the person who always livened up any situation by asking the question that made people laugh. She always asked about my staff's families and remembered birthdays and anniversaries. Susie was very talented and had a strong team spirit that she transferred to me.

One day, Susie and some of the other team members discovered an abandoned file drawer. They found several old hats, including a fur hat with a tail. Wearing the hats, they entered my office and sat down as if nothing were happening. I stared at them, bewildered.

"Jylla, lighten up!" Susie said to me as everyone burst out laughing. I was so stunned that I, too, could only laugh. Although it was hard in the beginning, I began to embrace her high spirits as a welcome respite from the challenging tasks of the job. I even allowed her to build free time for me on my calendar so that I could have the opportunity to do things I needed to do for myself.

Susie is definitely a high *I.* With her spirit and my focus on detail, we blended into a great team. To this day, when I need a "pick-me-upper," I call or email Susie. Her wonderful *I* spirit is with me always.

COACHABLE MOMENTS

As a result of my relationship with Susie, my DiSC® training, and my work as a coach, I find it necessary to respond to life differently. The better I understand how to react to people based on their behavior, the deeper and more productive are the relationships I have been able to establish. The DiSC® assessment provides a common language and a nonthreatening approach to working with and building relationships with people. At the same time, it levels the playing field because it allows us to focus on the common characteristics that make us human, rather than on the differences. DiSC® is a validated, research-based assessment that transcends diversity and provides commonality through style.

Once you understand your style, the challenge is to accept it and work with it. I have coached several people who thought of themselves as "people-persons," only to discover that they were anything but. I have worked with people who thought they were extremely conscientious, only to discover that they were more interested in cooperating with others than in digging deep to find the solution.

This is another area in which working with a coach can be extremely valuable. As you work through the process of dissecting your behavior style and analyzing the behavior of those in your environment, your coach will help you identify the patterns. The coach can help you bridge the gaps between all of the behavior styles in your environment—coachable moments—while helping to keep you focused, motivated, and moving toward the goals you've established.

Don Cipriano of Cipriano Training and Development, Inc. succinctly identified personal profile classical patterns with the following one-line descriptions:

"D" Profiles

Developer	"Watch out, here I come!"
Results oriented	"What's the bottom line?"
Inspirational	"Am I going to help you!"
Creative	"We need to have this perfect yesterday."

"I" Profiles

Promoter	"Do I have a deal for you!"
Persuader	"This is made for you!"

| Counselor | "All you need is love!" |
| Appraiser | "So you'll buy, if you're assured that . . ." |

"S" Profiles

Specialist	"Here is the final product."
Agent	"How can I help?"
Investigator	"How do you know that's right?"
Achiever	"My goal is . . ."

"C" Profiles

Objective thinker	"The facts in this matter seem to be . . ."
Perfectionist	"Do it right or don't do it at all!"
Practitioner	"The path of least resistance is . . ."

Attitude and behavior go hand-in-hand as critical Leadership Assets™. I often think of them as my BeAttitudes, a way to maintain *conscious* and *intentional* focus, as annotated in various books of the Bible.

> ➢ Be Content
> ➢ Be Courteous
> ➢ Be Thou Diligent
> ➢ Be Ye Doers
> ➢ Be Thou Faithful
> ➢ Be Ye Followers
> ➢ Be Glad
> ➢ Be of Good Courage
> ➢ Be Kindly "Affectioned"
> ➢ Be Sober
> ➢ Be Strong
> ➢ Be Zealous

These guiding principles keep me focused on the positive energy I need to leverage attitude and behavior as assets on my leadership journey.

THE FINAL THOUGHT . . . ATTITUDE AND BEHAVIOR

Your attitude (the external reflection of your feelings) and your behavior (how you act or respond in any given situation) are two major factors impacting your future, from the ability to progress in your career to your ability to have healthy and happy relationships. The great thing about attitude and behavior is that you have a choice. The moment you choose to have both a positive attitude and to exercise self-control, you determine the course of your future. This is true personal power!

Exhibit an affirmative Attitude and purposeful Behavior!

ATTITUDE AND BEHAVIOR

LESSONS LEARNED (NUGGETS)

1 _____
2 _____
3 _____

CHECKLIST

- ☐ 1 Thinks with a positive mental attitude
- ☐ 2 Understands attitude preference
- ☐ 3 Controls attitude triggers
- ☐ 4 Inspires and attracts others
- ☐ 5 Handles difficult situations with minimal stress
- ☐ 6 Masters personal behavior
- ☐ 7 Consciously flexes behavior
- ☐ 8 Reads and understands others' behavior
- ☐ 9 Approaches situations with attitude and behavior balance
- ☐ 10 Integrates and frames behavior during changing dynamics
- ☐ 11 Strives to shift focus to self responses in assessing behavior
- ☐ 12 Advocates for understanding behavior to strengthen communication

___ *Total*

ACTIONS PLANNED   COMPLETION DATE

1 _____   _____
2 _____   _____
3 _____   _____
4 _____   _____
5 _____   _____

BARRIERS/BLIND SPOTS

1 _____
2 _____
3 _____

ACHIEVEMENTS

1 _____
2 _____
3 _____

Change is an inevitability of life. It fosters your growth and development while fueling the sources of energy. The challenge is to "be prepared." Understanding the process of bridging gaps as you end an event, travel through, and start anew is the best approach for welcoming change in your life.

CHANGE

"Let Go and Let God." We know these words so well, but putting our faith in them is a challenge for us all . . . How confident we feel, how smoothly life unfolds, when we see that we have choices, and that nothing we value is at risk!

SUSAN L. TAYLOR
Senior Vice President and Editorial Director, *Essence* Magazine
"Letting God," *Essence* Magazine, September, 1998

When we accept the fact that change is ever-present, then we won't be surprised when it happens. As a matter of fact, the more flexible and fluid we are willing to be, the more prepared we are to handle change. Sometimes it is the season for positive change, such as a promotion or a new relationship. Or it can be the time for difficult change, such as a business deal falling through or the cancellation of a class you needed this semester. Ultimately, change fosters growth and development. But does that make it any easier to handle?

One of the changes most frequently occurring in the business world today is corporate reorganization. For community or service organizations, the correlation might be a change in the board of directors that results in a unilateral decision to reorganize. For entrepreneurs, it's a client who changes the scope of the work mere days before the deliverable dates.

If you are not a member of the team working behind the scenes on the "reorg," or if you failed to anticipate your new board's direction or your client's propensity to change his or her mind, you might not know about the change until the day it is announced. At that moment, you realize that the business or organization, as you have known it, will end. There will be shifts in strategy, management team transitions, and department realignments. There will be a series of meetings, building new teams, a determination of what's lost as a result of the reorganization, and a scramble to see what needs to be done to plug the holes. If a move of offices is required, there's that period in which you're adjusting to your new environment, maybe even to a new support staff.

After I made the decision to leave IBM to start my own company, I had second thoughts until I had lunch with a former colleague I respected tremendously. Don Jones made the transition from IBM into other very successful opportunities. He shared with me both the positive and negative aspects of transition, perspectives I had not considered before. I learned a critical lesson during our meeting: The presence of a support network when dealing with change can help you make the transition. Change, then, can feel liberating.

For others, surviving change and searching for new opportunities feels like being stuck in quicksand. They don't have the right skills; they don't communicate with or contribute to their new team; they have a poor attitude. It's time for an attitude check! To make the shift from negative to positive, one must quickly grab a rope or seek a new direction, such as learning something new. You must transform the new opportunity into a blessing. During the early phases, it is imperative that you do your homework, which includes understanding the dynamics of the new team, its behavior styles and expectations, the nuances of your new environment, and the communications processes.

Which attitude about change is most closely aligned with yours? Liberated or stuck? If you're stuck in quicksand, what are you doing about it?

THE COACH APPROACH

How do you really feel about change? What are the internal shifts you must make in order to "go with the flow"? How can you bridge the gap from the old to the new? Where can you contribute? What role can you serve? How can you become a positive force?

David Samuel, a highly regarded strategist and expert in customer service management and digital technology, discussed "rapid learning process" as a new survival skill during a presentation at the Black Management Conference for Northwestern University's Kellogg Graduate School. His presentation, which I read on his Web site, re-fueled my deep-rooted passion for lifelong learning. It was a powerful reminder that it is crucial to plan for the inevitable events in our lives. A *conscious* and *intentional* approach is to be a disciple of learning and a master of navigating changes in the rapid-fire manner in which we are confronted. Being a lifelong learner is the Coach Approach to preparation for the constantly changing environment in which we live. What are you currently doing that *consciously* and *intentionally* fulfills this aspect of change preparedness?

In the workbook used in a "Managing Transitions Seminar," developed by Inscape Publishing and adapted from the work of William Bridges, Ph.D., change is defined as an *external* process and transitions are *internal*; they are the "gradual psychological processes that we undergo in response to changes that occur in the world around us." Being able to manage transitions requires that you probe your understanding of your circumstances, bridge the gap, and then determine what actions are needed on the other side. Using discovery questioning allows you to see the bigger picture and then to focus on your new beginning.

One additional note: don't internalize what you're thinking or feeling during the process of change. Decide what type of support network you need. Look around you. If it isn't there, create it. Ask for help; ask your networks to start working on your behalf. Most importantly, avoid crying wolf every other day as you try to find your way through the strange new forest. It is important that you establish a solid foundation with your support team; they must know you well enough to be able to distinguish between a serious need for help and one of those "here we go again" complaints.

This would be a good time for you to do an assessment, such as "Managing Work Expectations," which could help you zero in on your areas of resistance before you get off track. It would be appropriate to seek guidance through a "Managing Transitions" coaching session or seminar and to diligently complete the journaling process. Change also invites the opportunity to employ again the behavior "flex" approach.

THE ROLE OF STRESS

Stress is a partner to change. Under stress, *dominance/director* people act without thinking. They just want to get it done. They not only break glass, they also shatter it. *Influence/presenter* styles deflect with humor. They change the focus. The *conscientiousness/strategist* will retreat to the details, the numbers, the statistics. They will procrastinate. The *steadiness/mediator* vents and flexes to a *dominance* behavior style. When they have tolerated as much as they care to, they make the shift. Ever heard someone say "I've never seen her act like that before"? That's behavior style in action. Understand your behavior with the "Coping and Stress Profile®" identified in Appendix B.

MY STORY

How did I decide to make the change in my life? What were the major triggers? What did I do to prepare myself? How did it all get started?

One of my major discoveries in graduate school was *Black Enterprise* Magazine. I was attracted to the cover of the magazine, which had the face of a black person making great strides in business. Inside were more stories about businesses owned or managed by prosperous and inspiring individuals around the nation. This was a new source of information for me. My aperture expanded. Suddenly I could see new possibilities.

I continued to subscribe to the magazine throughout my corporate career. I marveled at the successes, logged the advice, and dreamed of one day owning a business and working for myself. In 1997, I had the opportunity to participate in *Black Enterprise*'s Technology Summit. Shortly thereafter, I appointed myself IBM's executive liaison to *Black Enterprise*. I worked to build partnerships and alliances in conjunction with Evangeline Costa, who was one of the magazine's sales executives.

A couple of years later, during the *Black Enterprise* Entrepreneur's Conference, I had the opportunity to host an IBM-sponsored breakfast for the CEOs of the nation's top African-American businesses. With more than sixty of my idols and role models in the room, I announced that I was the long-lost daughter of Earl G. Graves, chairman and CEO of Earl G. Graves, Ltd. After what seemed like five minutes of dead silence, I explained that he had been my father *image* for business since 1978 when I first read the magazine. Everyone breathed a sigh of relief, especially Mr. Graves; then we all had a good laugh.

So often we affect people's lives in ways we may not realize. Although my vision of being an entrepreneur, nurtured by *Black Enterprise* Magazine, started early in my career, it took several events to propel me to shift from believing that I could be an entrepreneur to *knowing* that I *must*.

My last job at IBM was the position of vice president and client executive for a major retail account. I earned a strong and positive reputation as an executive and business leader. I was at the top of my game. Working on autopilot.

In January of that year, my oldest brother, Julius Moore Jr., was in a car accident. His injuries later resulted in his death at the age of forty-seven. The memory of his futile struggle for survival in the intensive care unit still haunts me. Yet, the memory of the response by Ralph Martino of IBM and Jerry Miller at Sears sets the benchmark for corporate leaders with spirit and soul. On the Saturday before my brother's funeral, I accepted an honorary doctorate degree from Livingstone College, my undergraduate alma mater. I use the title "Dr." today because my brother would have liked that. I just wish I could have shared the moment with him. The tragedy of my brother's death had a great impact on my life and forced me to rethink seriously my values and my life's purpose.

A couple of months later, IBM announced a dramatic change in its benefits plan. On the one hand, I fully understood and applauded the financial decision the company was making. On the other, the change, which impacted my retirement plan, presented me with a choice. Did I want to continue "doing" the jobs that would eventually include the possibility of my "retiring on the job," or did I want to find and pursue an opportunity that rallied my spirits and renewed my passion for "being" my life's work?

After the announcement about the benefits plan, there was another hurdle. I struggled with the influx of new services leadership. My vision for the business was out of sync with the decision makers. I wanted to move faster to structure and organize the marketing, sales, and service efforts than the company was ready. With my *DC* behavior at an all-time high, I wanted it done "my way." This is an example of Dr. Lois Frankel's fifth of eight career derailment factors: difficulty working with authority. (See Chapter 6 on Performance for the list of the other seven.) I was at a fork in the road, and I opted out of IBM.

My attitude and behavior, in hindsight, demonstrated all the symptoms of burnout. I was at the crossroads of my professional and personal life. I felt angry and torn. The close proximity between my brother's death and the changes at IBM brought me to this juncture. I was being forced to wrestle with and learn how to *manage transitions*, to adjust psychologically to the changes going on around me. I had to self-reflect and analyze what all these changes meant to me; I had to redefine what it meant to live a purposeful life. Because change ultimately fosters our growth, it became a defining moment.

Fortunately, I was able to have some downtime and enjoy the many elements of my life that had been neglected. I was beeper-less, agenda-less and clueless about what would evolve next. I spent time with my daughter, traveled, read, relaxed, cleaned house, and cleaned out closets.

I reentered the working world for what seemed to be an exciting opportunity. It turned out to be the shortest job tenure in my entire career. I spent forty-five days as president of an e-commerce solution company at the height of the e-commerce hysteria. But I quickly learned that the title really didn't give me the option to call the shots. Once again, I opted out.

PUTTING A STAKE IN THE GROUND

It is important to find humor in life, which is often difficult when in the midst of difficulties. Thinking about my situation reminds me of a story my Uncle Clint, who lived in New York City, once shared:

> *An intoxicated man once called him to ask for a ride home.*
> *"Where are you?" Uncle Clint asked.*
> *"At the corner of walk and don't walk," he responded.*

I was standing on the same street corner at this point in my journey and was trying to find *my* north. It was a classic coachable moment. That experience forced me to put a stake in the ground. It made me acknowledge that I wanted to own, manage, and be the president and chief executive officer of my own business. I decided that I no longer wanted to work for anyone else and needed to venture out into the entrepreneurial universe. It was one of the riskiest decisions of my life. I was stuck on the sidelines until I *intentionally* made the decision to get back in the game with my own rules. These rules included making choices about how I would spend my time, about doing work that was my passion, and about the skills that I could tap into that would provide the foundation for developing a business. With the options and the possibilities on the storyboard, I created and launched Crystal Stairs, Inc.

Change doesn't occur overnight. The time that it takes to go through the *transition* process varies from situation to situation. I think that my transition involved reconciling with emotional events in a way that allowed my intuition to align with my vision for life. At that point, I stopped opting, and I headed north.

NOTHING STAYS THE SAME

Throughout my IBM career, I accepted change as a normal course of business, almost as common as a "change order form" or the regular shifting of teams. In IBM, every year there were major changes: an announcement of a new product, a new organization structure, a revolving door of managers and teams. One of the best books I've read on change is *Who Moved My Cheese?* by Spencer Johnson, M.D. The book provides a simple yet powerful case for change. It's very important to know when to close one door and walk through another, when to venture in search of something new. If mice and rats can figure out how to navigate a maze and keep moving, then we, too, must figure it out.

For me, change meant transitioning from a successful corporate executive position, with its support systems and perks, to becoming CEO, better known as the "Chief Everything Officer," in my own entrepreneurial venture. Bridging that gap felt like going into a tunnel with no visible light at the end. It wasn't until I began to *create* that new beginning—a beginning for which I had total control, ability, skills, passion, and flexibility to choose my work and life components—that I found *my* cheese. At the same time, as I dictated and managed my time, I had to make sure that I continued to set goals and objectives. I understood the level of quality and service agreements that were important to maintain with my clients and to brand the services of my new business. But I was building upon other powerful changes that had occurred in my life:

➢ From IBM to Crystal Stairs
➢ From member to international president
➢ From single to married with child
➢ From child care to elder care

Major changes continue to occur. When things change, life is never the same. There is a void. There is a need to bridge the gaps from what was to what is. In times of change, I turn to Ecclesiastes 2:3: "For everything there is a season, and a purpose for every matter."

COACHABLE MOMENT

I had a client who was a "24/7" executive for twenty-two years, thanks to her pager and cell phone. Three weeks before the Christmas holiday, she received notice that she would be impacted by a work-force reduction. During our initial conversation, she attacked the injustice and timing of her layoff and struggled with the fairness of her treatment. However, my discovery questioning with her zeroed in on what she would do with the extra gift of time that she had been given. She accepted the challenge. This is what Amy reported:

> *In honor of my beloved mom (who's been in heaven for sixteen years), I planned a gathering with a few of HER friends in my home! I had them over for lunch, an afternoon snack, and then for dinner, too! We spent several hours reminiscing, joking, and giggling, and we even got to do crafts! These ladies were a few of Mom's best friends who occasionally still keep in touch with us and who we only see at weddings (or funerals). I was so glad I got to spend quality time with them.*
>
> *Second, I spent an entire day (while the kids were at school) preparing the Christmas menu. My aunt, sister, and I got together at*

my sister's, and we made (literally) hundreds of tamales, all from scratch! It took us approximately nine to ten hours to make about 450 of them . . . In the long process of kneading the cornmeal, cooking the meat, stuffing and wrapping the cornhusks, etc., we enjoyed each other's company and had heart-pouring conversations! (I hadn't participated in making tamales since my mom was alive.)

Third, I truly enjoyed participating in planning the sixth grade holiday party! We schemed up some real fun games and stuffed the kids with tons of treats. They seemed to have enjoyed the party. . . just being able to mingle with friends in a 'festive' atmosphere was their definition of fun.

My goal is to start classes (at the outplacement center) next week . . . I'm working on a target list of companies that I'm interested in looking into. I also am contemplating "switching gears" and perhaps consider(ing) a different career. I'm open to new options.

It is clear that once my client embraced change and altered her attitude about her situation, it turned out to be a wonderful opportunity for her to do things she had previously been unable to do. Amy, thanks for the great lessons in living a *conscious* and *intentional* life!

THE FINAL THOUGHT . . . CHANGE

If we think of change as a gift, and watch it unfold as if pulling the wrapping paper off the present, we might be pleasantly and joyfully surprised by its contents.

Always be prepared to Ride the Crests of Change!

CHANGE

LESSONS LEARNED (NUGGETS)
1 _____
2 _____
3 _____

CHECKLIST
- ❑ 1 Welcomes change
- ❑ 2 Prepares to handle change
- ❑ 3 Views change as an opportunity to grow
- ❑ 4 Finds "nuggets" in change
- ❑ 5 Understands new expectations
- ❑ 6 Celebrates the old and "lets go"
- ❑ 7 Demonstrates a willingness to change approach based on feedback
- ❑ 8 Advocates for lifelong learning
- ❑ 9 Envisions the big picture
- ❑ 10 Successfully bridges gaps
- ❑ 11 Remains flexible when policies and/or procedures change
- ❑ 12 Handles change-related stress

___ *Total*

ACTIONS PLANNED   COMPLETION DATE
1 _____   _____
2 _____   _____
3 _____   _____
4 _____   _____
5 _____   _____

BARRIERS/BLIND SPOTS
1 _____
2 _____
3 _____

ACHIEVEMENTS
1 _____
2 _____
3 _____

> Dynamic communication is two-way communication. It is the clarity of the message as well as the listener's ability to receive it. To be a dynamic communicator, you must also be an effective listener. It is sensitivity to and management of the messenger's chosen format to deliver the message.

COMMUNICATION

"To excel in communications, you must take responsibility for what you say as well as what they hear."

IVY BENNETT
Assistant Vice President, Allstate Insurance Company

Communication is generally defined as the giving or exchanging of ideas. The traditional modes include talking to someone in person, writing memos and/or letters, and talking on the telephone. The technology explosion created additional communication tools that are now a major part of our lives: cellular telephones, pagers, conference calls, voice mail, and email. For those on the Crystal Stairs Leadership Journey, mastery of effective communication as an asset is essential.

Effective communication means being an effective listener and delivering concise messages. Effective listening is more than just *hearing*. It is the ability to *hear* the underlying message. It is the ability to interpret other cues, such as body language, whether visual, auditory, or virtual. Unfortunately, with so much information vying for our attention in so many formats, we tend to filter out the message or change the intended meaning of what we hear. The *conscious* and *intentional* leader develops an approach to listening that is appropriate to any situation.

THE COACH APPROACH

This is an exercise that I often use in my training sessions:

Divide into groups of two. For two minutes, the first person must talk while the second listens without saying anything. The two people should maintain eye contact. When the first person is finished, the second will talk without interruption while maintaining eye contact. What is the result?

Hopefully, participants became more aware of their listening skills. Because of the way we traditionally have communicated, remaining quiet for two minutes is hard. We're used to interjecting our thoughts, either verbally or mentally. Think about the times you "half-listen." Have you agreed to do something requested by your child, spouse, or a colleague because you weren't really paying attention? Staying in the moment takes practice. Let's try another exercise:

Conduct a thirty-minute conversation with a child. Listen intently, and limit your responses. Your questions and responses should be careful, nonthreatening, and nonjudgmental and should be made in the manner in which you would want an adult to communicate with you. We sometimes take for granted that it is okay to use children as a communication punching bag. Challenge yourself to listen and respond as you would like others to listen and respond to you. What did you learn from the exercises?

There are five listening styles: Appreciative, Empathetic, Comprehensive, Discerning, and Evaluative. For more information, see Appendix B for information about the Personal Listening Profile®.

STAYING IN THE MOMENT

When I provide ground rules in a training session, I usually refer to the *New York Times'* best-seller *FISH!* by Stephen Lundin, Ph.D., Harry Paul, and John Christensen. The story presents four principles essential to the foundation of *conscious* and *intentional* communications:

➢ Choose your attitude.
➢ Play.
➢ Make their day.
➢ Be present.

To help the audience stay in the moment, I insist that cell phones and pagers be turned off. I not only talk about communications, but it is also my goal to *communicate* in a way that is humorous and makes the training session fun. Given my high *DC* behavior, this is a challenge. I have to work at it. I use personal stories and share my experiences in order to relate to the audience and create light moments. We play. I insist that each person do something special for someone else during the course of the day. Finally, I seek engagement, interaction, and a positive attitude for learning.

One of the stories I share about communication involves my daughter. We were sitting in the Cincinnati airport's Delta Crown Room Club in January. My daughter loved to travel, and she loved looking at all of the people in the room. While we waited for our plane, a woman walked by in a white furry coat. My daughter got very excited. "Mommy!" she cried out in her loud, three-year-old voice, "Where's the doggie going?" It was one of those moments in which I witnessed the communication process through the eyes of a child: She was very excited, she was in the moment, she wanted to go play, and she probably made that woman's day. Thank goodness the woman smiled and responded with a positive attitude. Thank goodness the woman understood that a child communicates in a very honest, nonjudgmental, and impetuous manner.

THE LINK BETWEEN BEHAVIOR AND COMMUNICATION

When working on a team, remember that each member will have a unique style of communication, usually tied to his or her behavior. Let's focus again on DiSC® behavior as it relates to communication:

COMMUNICATION AND DISC® BEHAVIOR	
D	Takes control of building the image. Driven to win, they immediately seize upon a challenge, whatever it may be.
I	Creates ways to help; tries to build team spirit in order to win. At the conclusion, they often anoint themselves as the winners.
S	Sits on the sidelines and watches the activity; they engage and participate only when invited.
C	Usually decides in advance what will be built, how it will be built, and what equations are needed to win.

Teams who understand the dynamics of behavior and communication style achieve greater success.

COACHABLE MOMENT

As a manager, it sometimes falls to you to share tough messages with people. This requires a special skill. I had a manager who one day pulled me aside and told me I needed to slow down and focus on communicating with the peer-management team. Apparently, my *DC* behavior style was getting in the way. It was a coachable moment for me, a moment when I had to step outside of myself, listen to his *truth-saying*, and deal with someone else's perception of my behavior. Of course, he could have kept his thoughts to himself. Or I could have responded to his frankness with attitude—and with plenty of it. But because he took the time to give me feedback on my management style, I was made aware of the need for *conscious* and *intentional* communication with all subsequent teams at an early point in my management career. Thanks, John Burkard!

In a later stage of my IBM career, I took the Myers Briggs Type Indicator Assessment. It revealed my personality style as *INTJ* (*introverted, intuitive, thinking,* and *judging* as contrasted with *extrovert, sensing, feeling, perceiving*). As an *INTJ*, I was a logical, orderly thinker with a preference for interacting with the world through an internal approach. The key for me was the confirmation that I was an introvert. That meant that I had to have purpose, parameters, and a welcoming environment before I opened up. This assessment confirmed something that I already knew about myself. But it also revealed my need to be more conscious about my struggle to be in the moment and to respond appropriately. I needed to become *conscious* and *intentional* about the who, what, when, where, and how of my communication with people.

In my training sessions, I often share the fact that I am introverted, to the great surprise of many participants. A number of achievement-oriented individuals relate to the challenge of introversion, share their stories, and ask for help. It has made me more sensitive to the impact of personality styles on communication. I tell my audiences they must search for and utilize communication techniques that enable them to be (who they need to be) in the moment, whether they are introverts or extroverts. Let me clarify one point: There is a difference between personality and behavior. Personality, a person's character and traits, is innate. Behavior, on the other hand, is both situational and environmental. It is based on choice.

How do I motivate my introverted self? How do I energize myself? To do that, I see myself walking through the process; I envision the end game. I establish my communication objectives and plan the results. My personal mantra is to focus on "showtime." "Showtime" is when I am standing in front of a group and conducting a training session or delivering a speech. I am the center of focus, with an audience of twenty or two thousand, onstage at the microphone. It's quiet. All eyes are on me.

I pay attention to my personal appearance because it also communicates my "presence" business card. My look is recognizable; my image is part of my brand. My former leader, Bob LaBant, used to buy a new tie for every big presentation. It was his way of motivating himself. It is a little more difficult to purchase a new suit for every presentation, so instead I sometimes buy myself a new pin. I learned from Bob how to establish symbolic celebrations; even small pins can motivate us to push beyond our comfort zone so we can communicate effectively. It's showtime!

COMMUNICATION TOOLS

There are so many ways to communicate today that it can be mind-boggling. From telephones, cellular phones, pagers, and two-way radios to email, voice mail, faxes, and instant text messaging, we have potentially unlimited access to each other, round-the-clock if necessary. It is startling to see people on the telephone any and everywhere: driving their cars, riding the train, pushing grocery carts. Even in the library, one hears the familiar beep of pagers or the musical ring of cellular phones. I have even heard cellular telephones ringing in church on Sunday mornings!

Even though we can have unlimited access to people, we have to be aware that in addition to our intended audience there is an unintended audience. The *conscious* and *intentional* leader recognizes the importance of electronic etiquette. What is electronic etiquette? Technology has raced far ahead of evolving rules of governance, but there are some basic guidelines that I think are important. Coach Judy Irving shared some of them with me:

- ➤ Your cellular telephones and pagers should be on vibrate in public places.

- ➤ Never allow your phones or pagers to ring or beep at the movies; in school; at your church, synagogue, or mosque; at the museum; at the library, or while eating lunch or dinner in a restaurant.

- ➤ Promptly return pages and voice mail. If you're going to be in meetings or out of town on business and unable to return a call, make sure you change your voice-mail message to indicate that.

- ➤ Promptly respond to all emails in a concise and professional manner. An email is an example of your professional correspondence.

- ➤ It is also important to brand yourself. Add color, italics, or bold type. It is very simple to do but also a way to make your content stand out.

- ➤ At the bottom of your business emails, include a signature line that includes your name, title, telephone number, fax number, email address, and even your mailing address.

- ➤ Be sensitive about passing along forwarded email messages. Having people sort through fifty different forwarded address lists before getting to the actual contents is both unprofessional and a waste of their time. You should copy and paste the relevant information into a new message before sending it.

- ➤ If you prefer not to receive forwarded stories and jokes, ask that your name be removed from the distribution list.

- ➤ At the start of conference calls, make sure all of the participants are introduced.

- ➤ On a conference call, never discuss information that is not intended for the entire group, even if you think everyone else has hung up.

- ➤ Never put a person on a speakerphone without permission.

FOCUSING THE MESSAGE

The influx of the Internet as a communication tool also requires succinct messaging. That's when I rely on my "storyboard." To help me clarify my point, whether by email or in a two-hour presentation, I take a sheet of paper and divide it into sixteen squares. I then list the key points and order the presentation. It helps to focus the message, organize the critical points, and consolidate the input in an orderly manner.

How well do you come across? How authentic do you sound? How effective are you? These questions and others will start you down the pathway of effective communication. The Certified Communicator Program© published by Coach U also provides a tremendous vehicle to assess your effectiveness in communicating. I highly recommend it as an anchor in the establishment of your growth objectives.

CERTIFIED COMMUNICATOR PROGRAM

Circle the 1 or 3 if the word matches, 2 if combination of the words.

1. How well do you come across?
These are how others would likely describe your communication style.

1	Loud	1 2 3	Quiet
2	Fast/slow	1 2 3	Natural
3	Charged up/down	1 2 3	Neutral
4	Complain	1 2 3	Pleased
5	Flat	1 2 3	Expressive
6	Speak at	1 2 3	Share with
7	Heavy/significant	1 2 3	Light
8	Pedantic	1 2 3	Simple
9	Suspicious	1 2 3	Friendly/trusting
10	Rigid	1 2 3	Flexible

2. How well do you listen?
How well do you hear what is being said, and not said?

11	Listen hard	1 2 3	Be with
12	Hear info/facts	1 2 3	Hear it all
13	Wait for evidence	1 2 3	Trust inklings
14	Acquires info	1 2 3	Learns
15	Listens passively	1 2 3	Knows what to listen for
16	Prepares response	1 2 3	Hears the person
17	Doubting	1 2 3	Accepting
18	Interrupts	1 2 3	Prompts
19	One thing at a time	1 2 3	Can handle multiple inputs
20	Hears 10–90%	1 2 3	Hears 90–100%

© 1998 Coach U, Inc.

continued . . .

3. How well do you articulate?
How well are you understood?

21	Talks at	1 2 3	Contextualizes
22	Lectures	1 2 3	Educates
23	Rambles	1 2 3	Succinct
24	Clichés	1 2 3	Messages
25	Jargon	1 2 3	"English"
26	Rote	1 2 3	Personalizes
27	General terms	1 2 3	Specific terms
28	Holds back	1 2 3	Says it all
29	Convoluted	1 2 3	Clear
30	Limited vocabulary	1 2 3	Extensive vocabulary

4. What do you converse about?
What do you focus on and talk about with others?

31	Symptoms	1 2 3	Source of the problem
32	The negative	1 2 3	The positive
33	The past	1 2 3	The present/how things are
34	Coulds & shoulds	1 2 3	What you really want
35	Reactions	1 2 3	Chosen responses
36	Swaps info	1 2 3	Dances
37	Responds to facts	1 2 3	Gets the gist
38	The "What"	1 2 3	The "Who"
39	Facts	1 2 3	Concepts
40	Others	1 2 3	Yourselves

5. How well do you converse?
How often do you have fluid, two-way conversations?

41	Repeats/echoes	1 2 3	Improves phrasing
42	Reactive	1 2 3	Responsive
43	Speak (half-duplex)	1 2 3	Speak *and* listen (full)
44	Unaware of mood	1 2 3	Matches mood
45	Distracted	1 2 3	Attentive
46	Confrontive	1 2 3	Evoking
47	Delayed response	1 2 3	Immediate response
48	Adds a spin	1 2 3	Adds no spin
49	Non-sequitor	1 2 3	Tracks/follows
50	Pepper w/ questions	1 2 3	Clarifies what was said

6. How authentic do you sound?
How real are you and how real do you sound?

51	Pretentious	1 2 3	Non-pretentious
52	Puffs up people	1 2 3	Is accurate with praise
53	Sneaky	1 2 3	Forthright, forthcoming
54	Dishonest	1 2 3	Completely honest
55	Overstates	1 2 3	Accurately states
56	Performs	1 2 3	Relates
57	Knows it all	1 2 3	Seeks to learn
58	Is "affected"	1 2 3	Real
59	Full of it	1 2 3	Legitimate
60	Ingenuine/insincere	1 2 3	Genuine

7. How big are you?
How flexible, respectful, and generous are you?

61	Critical	1 2 3	Constructive
62	Excludes people	1 2 3	Includes people
63	One-ups	1 2 3	Endorses
64	Disrespectful	1 2 3	Respectful
65	Result-driven	1 2 3	Person-oriented
66	Judges	1 2 3	Tolerant
67	Pushes agenda	1 2 3	Shares your views
68	"On"	1 2 3	Not "on"
69	Rigid	1 2 3	Open
70	Digs	1 2 3	Builds a person up

8. How mature are you?
What does your communication style tell others about you?

71	Hesitant	1 2 3	Confident
72	Fearful	1 2 3	Goes for it
73	Speaks haltingly	1 2 3	Fluid
74	Repeats/mimics	1 2 3	Synthesizes
75	Gossips	1 2 3	Doesn't gossip
76	Childish	1 2 3	Adult
77	Blames	1 2 3	Owns
78	Clueless	1 2 3	Speaks with wisdom
79	Speaks from theory	1 2 3	Speaks from experience
80	Righteous	1 2 3	Compassionately accurate

9. How free are you of Communication Blocks?
What's holding back your effectiveness as a communicator?

81	Compulsive talker	1 2 3	Listens more than talks
82	Personally needy	1 2 3	Has plenty, a reserve
83	Adrenalined/up	1 2 3	Present
84	Ignorant	1 2 3	Informed/educated
85	Toxic personality	1 2 3	Clean and healthy as a person
86	Attached to past	1 2 3	Creating a future
87	Stressed	1 2 3	Calm
88	Unconscious	1 2 3	Conscious/aware
89	Blind spots	1 2 3	360-degree view
90	Conspiratorial	1 2 3	Cooperative

10. How effective are you?
How good are you at producing results?

91	Hints at	1 2 3	Asks directly
92	Silent/says little	1 2 3	Speaks up/requests
93	Dealing in past	1 2 3	Dealing in the present
94	Immediate gratification	1 2 3	Long-term investor
95	Win-oriented	1 2 3	Win-win oriented
96	Problem-oriented	1 2 3	Solution-oriented
97	Book knowledge	1 2 3	Street smarts
98	Shares a goal	1 2 3	Inspires with a vision
99	Bounces around	1 2 3	Sees/gets right to problem
100	Talks about stuff	1 2 3	Is "for" stuff

COACHABLE MOMENT

A vivid, coachable moment that I have heard about involved electronic etiquette and a corporate executive. After a conference call, he stayed on the line to discuss some personnel issues with another colleague. Unbeknownst to him, not everyone had hung up. The personnel information he shared during that call became public knowledge. It was a lesson learned for everyone involved.

Management 101 reminds us of the "sunshine rule" for communication. Approach all communication—what we say as well as what we write—as if it might show up on the front page of a newspaper the next morning.

MAKING YOUR POINT

Some people are masterful storytellers with full command of the English language. They usually are exceptional speakers. Since the 1970s, I have been a great fan of motivational speaker Patricia Russell-McCloud, J.D. Not only is she articulate and direct, her presentations are powerful. Her book *A Is for Attitude, An Alphabet for Living* provides lessons critical to understanding how to live a fulfilling life. She channels her communication expertise to remind us all to "Learn to live with Attitude and Courage, to tap your Genius and Brainpower, to fight for Justice and Truth, to take Risks and develop a brilliant Vision, and to use this Know-How to grab Life Now." What power! What command of communication through the written and the spoken word!

MAKING THE NETWORK WORK

Once you've mastered your communication assets, how can you best use them? Use them to meet people, to build relationships, and to network. The most effective networking relationships are based on a spirit of mutual value, rather than on personal gain and benefit. Remember to separate business and personal relationships. There is a distinction between a friend and an associate. That becomes clear when you observe the manner in which someone responds to you (don't forget body language). Because relationships are two-way streets, be sensitive to how the relationship is defined. When communicating that you are acquaintances, does the person claim to be your long-lost friend, or is it a business-network relationship? Never "assume" that you know the depth of a relationship unless it has been discussed. Be cautious.

Whatever the relationship, it is imperative that your personal principles not be compromised. Trust, integrity, and confidence are integral to building and nurturing successful relationships; these traits must become part of your heart and soul. People must be able to count on you to deliver what you promise.

George Fraser is the master of networking. His book *Success Runs In Our Race* is an excellent guide to developing the unique art of networking. His thought provoking dialogue has been tested over many years and he continues to espouse his belief that "the only networking that works is networking for the benefit of others." I would highly recommend participating in one of his sessions to learn and/or refine the communication asset of networking. In addition, invest in the Success Guides that he publishes for cities across the country as they provide the tools for doing the work of building and sustaining an economic network.

WHAT DO WE COMMUNICATE ABOUT OURSELVES?

Do we communicate who we are based on the work that we do? It is important to understand that titles come and go. For example, I was a vice president of IBM; now I'm president and chief executive officer of Crystal Stairs. I also was the Grand Basileus and international president of Zeta Phi Beta Sorority. I have since changed companies and changed titles. I no longer work for IBM and I am no longer Grand Basileus of Zeta Phi Beta Sorority. But did I change who I am?

It's important to understand and communicate what is innate and consistent about who you are. For me, that means that no matter what title precedes or follows my name, I will always be, and I only want to be, Jylla.

ANOTHER COACHABLE MOMENT

Don't forget to use the personal touch in your communication. For example, when you communicate with others by *celebrating what is,* you can add tremendous value to your business and personal relationships. Taking the time to acknowledge or to congratulate someone by sending an email is one way to stay in touch with them. Or you can go the next step by sending an electronic greeting (e-card). Better yet, you can send a handwritten note through the mail.

Acknowledging the birthdays and anniversaries of your friends and business associates is important. Set up an electronic reminder that will trigger greetings on certain dates.

Bob was the master of *celebrating what is*. He often sent flowers to the homes of his team members at the end of a difficult day or at the end of a challenging project. This strong message of support and appreciation was a Coachable Moment for me. Both Bob and public-relations consultant Terrie Williams, author of *The Personal Touch*, have been my *celebrating what is* "gurus" and I have learned a lot from them.

THE FINAL THOUGHT . . . COMMUNICATION

Communication is one of the most critical Leadership Assets™. It incorporates several other assets, and using it effectively can be the fuel for success. Expertise with standard and traditional forms of communication is expected. Our written and verbal communication must be impeccable. Now, add the new wares to your tool kit.

Communicate in a dynamic, essential, and effective manner!

COMMUNICATION

LESSONS LEARNED (NUGGETS)

1 _____
2 _____
3 _____

CHECKLIST

- ☐ 1 Communicates information accurately and precisely
- ☐ 2 Open to different points of view
- ☐ 3 Listens "in the moment" with good listening skills
- ☐ 4 Flex to communicate based on behavior styles
- ☐ 5 Excellent written communication skills
- ☐ 6 Excellent verbal communication skills
- ☐ 7 Concise and articulate in communicating key information
- ☐ 8 Uses humor and stories to relate messages
- ☐ 9 Makes the network work
- ☐ 10 Engages communication etiquette
- ☐ 11 Uses productive and appropriate communication tools
- ☐ 12 Communicates a personal brand

___ *Total*

ACTIONS PLANNED   COMPLETION DATE

1 _____   _____
2 _____   _____
3 _____   _____
4 _____   _____
5 _____   _____

BARRIERS/BLIND SPOTS

1 _____
2 _____
3 _____

ACHIEVEMENTS

1 _____
2 _____
3 _____

Treasuring everyone, irrespective of race, gender, ethnicity, sexual orientation, age, religion, and/or level of expertise is prizing diversity. It is based on the belief that this dynamic interaction will benefit all participants, as well as the bottom line.

DIVERSITY

We must focus on inclusion now more than ever. All of our employees' energy and knowledge must be utilized as we venture to compete in an increasing number of consumer markets. It is imperative that we reach our customers, our employees, and our business partners using inclusive diversity practices in all levels of the organization.

TEXANNA M. REEVES
Manager, Georgia-Pacific Corporation

Many corporations and businesses focus on diversity in response to public protests, employee actions, lawsuits, government intervention, or public pressure. However, the more leaders and individuals understand why diversity is valuable and how to demonstrate that value, the more potential there is for bottom-line success. From the standpoint of a *conscious* and *intentional* leader, prizing diversity means recognizing the importance of tapping into different cultures, lifestyles, generations, religious beliefs, traditions, experiences, skills, work styles, and thoughts. It is a way to protect the viability of your company or business. The challenge is to go from theory to practice, from the sidelines to center court.

Some people need a personal experience before it hits them that diversity is a business imperative. An IBM senior executive became a major advocate in the workplace for sensitivity to gender issues after the daughter of a close friend was sexually harassed at her company's event. That was his wake-up call. He also taught through example, by demonstrating to his peers the necessity of building a very talented and diverse team. Have you had your wake-up call?

MY "THREE-SIDED" STORY

The Corporate Side: I first participated on a diversity council while working for IBM in Detroit. Our charge was to identify high-potential employees within the company and to determine what training and skills were needed to help them advance. The council, which was a reflection of the company's early commitment to develop individual employee talent, later worked on a plan for the recruitment of minority vendors.

In the mid-'90s, IBM assembled eight executive task forces—one each for African-Americans, Asians, Hispanics, Native Americans, women, white males, gays and lesbians, and the disabled. The groups were charged with answering three questions: What is necessary to make your group feel welcome and valued at IBM? What can we do, in partnership with your group, to maximize your group's productivity? What can we do to influence your group's buying decisions so that IBM is seen as a solution provider? As a member of the Women's Task Force and a contributor to the African-American Task Force, I was pleased to help articulate and document what steps the company could take to demonstrate that it valued its employees and what it could do to target and better serve its diverse marketplace.

Spearheaded by Ted Childs, vice president of Worldwide Diversity for IBM, the task force initiative became a major spoke in the wheel of IBM's transformation. Task force participants and other employees began to witness the impact of their contributions to the process. A beneficial but unanticipated byproduct of their participation was that their careers also moved forward. Through the initiative, IBM was able to fill the pipeline with many qualified and talented individuals, and the numbers of diverse employees increased in key areas of leadership and influence.

The initiative also led to the establishment of affinity groups, organizations that come together based on special interests. Their goal is not to be divisive, but rather to address the specific needs of members.

Affinity groups became the vehicle to help develop the skills of individuals through formal programs, information sharing, mentoring, networking, and access to invited executive guests. Joined by a common mission—helping each other advance through the business pipeline—the groups provided opportunities for openness and sharing. The groups also broke the unspoken code that it was okay to associate with colleagues who were of like purpose.

The establishment of affinity groups demonstrated corporations' commitment to value and retain talent. The General Electric (GE) African-American Forum (AAF) was my introduction to the power of strengthening the business through support of an affinity group. When asked what GE was doing to recruit and retain diverse talent, Jack Welch, former CEO, challenged his executives. His response was a defining moment in my life. With the confidence of a true leader, he told the executives at the AAF meeting that as leaders, it was *their* responsibility, as much as his, to make it happen!

The Community Side: Wherever I traveled, I learned leadership skills that served as the wind at my back. In 1995, for example, I attended the Fourth United Nation's World Conference on Women in Beijing, China. The chance to join an assembly of women representing nongovernmental organizations from around the world was personally transforming. There were some language barriers, but our common purpose brought us together. Comparing the atrocities faced by some women to the blessings enjoyed by others was an awakening that will be forever etched in my mind. Because of our constitutional rights, our legal system, and our societal mores, we experience a high level of comfort in the United States. Such comfort is not afforded to all women around the world. We must continue the struggle for access to capital and human rights that can become the tickets to freedom for women who are still captives of injustice.

International assignments and internships are excellent ways to deepen your awareness and appreciation of different cultures. Military service is another approach. Even organizations at educational institutions, such as student alliances, provide opportunities to appreciate and prize diversity.

The Organization Side: Sororities and fraternities are a vital component of African-American culture, but I vehemently oppose any mental or physical hazing of aspirants who pledge them. Members of the class of 1976 at Livingstone College who chose to pledge had the right attitude. Despite the fact that we joined different organizations that were often competitive, we maintained our focus on education and supported one another. We networked with one another and learned to collaborate. Our goal was to provide better services in the community and more opportunities to spend time on community service and scholarship, the common denominator for all of the fraternities and sororities. Rather than be divisive in our efforts, we were one. We approached each opportunity to provide community service from the standpoint of succeeding together.

THE COACH APPROACH

Prizing diversity can help facilitate the development of untapped or unrecognized talent. We each can point to individuals in our careers who have helped us develop professionally. The process of coaching goes beyond mentoring. It helps you see your blind spots and gaps about diversity. Using laser focus and truth-saying, the Coach Approach allows you to zero in on development issues that may be holding you back. The coach can become the confidante with whom you share a dialogue about diversity. The coach will encourage you to find ways to broaden your professional and personal experiences, to get outside of your comfort zone, and eliminate a victim or entitlement mentality. From eating at different restaurants to attending festivals or celebrations, the emphasis is creating situations where you are challenged to think, learn, and grow.

The coach may encourage you to find ways to engage in dialogue with different groups of people, through forming or participating in diversity councils and affinity groups, attending community meetings, participating in multicultural business forums, or engaging in a candid exchange with your customers. In addition, the Discovering Diversity Profile® is an assessment noted in Appendix B that can help you objectively understand your level of awareness, knowledge, understanding, and acceptance, as well as your behavior related to diversity.

One other point: Make sure your Team 100™, discussed in the Teamwork chapter, also includes a multicultural mix of people.

DIVERSITY INSPECTION

Sometimes, when we look at the makeup of some corporations' executive teams, we think a game is being played. In the Fortune 500 circle, the team is usually all-white and all-male. Sometimes the teams have members who are related, which makes it difficult to believe that some families have so much talent that all of the siblings hold top slots in one company. It's easy to point to the inequality. What we have to recognize is that business decisions are not always based on merit. They are based on relationships. We should focus, therefore, not only on being able to stand on our own merit, but also on establishing important networks and relationships.

Occasionally, individuals who have been beneficiaries of diversity programs develop amnesia. They forget whose shoulders they stand upon, or whose blood, sweat, and tears paved the way and *continue* to pave the way for them. They live behind a mask and become wrapped up in the titles, the material benefits of the job, and the prospects for wealth. They have lost the sense of responsibility to give back, to reach out and pull someone else forward. For each of us who treasures our diverse world, that is a responsibility we should never forget; we must carry the load daily. We can't sit at the table with silent voices. We must choose our battles and then weigh in so that the doors that we've managed to open can remain open.

EMPLOYEE RELATIONS AND DIVERSITY

I once was asked to remove a sales representative from her territory. I suspected that performance was the issue, but she insisted her client was uncomfortable with the fact that she was a woman. The challenge was to separate legitimate performance issues from possible discriminatory acts. In a conversation with the employee, I discovered she was not effectively developing client relationships, which was key to mastering the position. In that instance, what steps would you take? What truth-saying is included in the conversation?

In another situation, a young female sales representative with clients in remote areas of the Midwest felt very comfortable with her clients and vice versa. At dinner one evening, her client used racial slurs during the conversation. She was surprised but maintained her composure well enough to close the deal. Still, she wondered how she should have responded. What would you have done? What conversations need to happen?

Sometimes, personal values and choices play a role, too. Recently, two African-American executives opted not to attend major meetings sponsored by their company because the meetings were being held on Martin Luther King Jr. Day, an optional company holiday. Their decision made a statement that resonated both ways. Companies need to be attuned to cultural sensitivities; employees have to make decisions about their value systems. What would you do if you were the employee? What would you do if you represented the company?

COACHABLE MOMENTS

There have been many coachable moments in which I had the opportunity to educate or be educated. I would like to share one in particular.

On the day my promotion to vice president at IBM was announced, I attended a luncheon sponsored by the IBM women's initiative marketing team in honor of Black History Month. We invited to Washington, D.C., approximately fifty women, primarily African-American business partners and clients from across the country. U. S. Secretary of Commerce Ron Brown was the keynote speaker, and he talked about his commitment to developing the continent of Africa. That a man who had achieved such stature would attempt to make a difference in Africa was very thought provoking to me. A month later, Brown was killed in a plane crash.

Reflecting on that moment with Secretary Brown, and on my participation with the IBM task forces, I realized that all of these endeavors were related. They were all part of the same continuum: to recognize the importance of diversity, to expand opportunities, to make a difference. The business imperative of diversity is more than the extension of a helping hand. It requires that we also give back.

In many companies, an individual has responsibility for sales and marketing to diverse clients. A company that makes the investment in broadening its market reach by targeting markets and delivering custom approaches to building customers for life represents true visionary leadership. Some of my role models have worked at many companies, continue to work at the company, or have moved to new ventures and opportunities. But these individuals and their work first captured my attention: Alvenia Rhea Albright, American Express; Warren Manns and Elizabeth Murphy, American Airlines; Jacquelyn Gates, Bell Atlantic; Elynor Williams, Sara Lee Inc.; Peter Campbell, Lotus; Lisa Cole, Nordstrom; Shirley Rivers, The Walt Disney Company; Ingrid Saunders-Jones, Coca-Cola Co.; Wayman Smith and Thelma Cook, Anheuser Busch; Toni Fay, AOL-Time Warner; and Wanda McKenzie of IBM.

Minority Business News USA is my constant source for current information on the world of Minority Business Enterprise and Diversity. Don McKneely, publisher, and Carol Daugherty Foster, editor, continue to raise the bar in reporting newsworthy stories that ignite ideas, spark new energy, and applaud companies and individuals who are diligently working to advance business relationships. Monthly, they live up to their mission statement "to be first and best at delivering business news and information affecting the minority community and its economic development."

THE FUTURE OF DIVERSITY

Recently, on a teleconference call with some of my Corporate Coach University International peers, a provocative question was asked: "Is diversity still an important issue?" Unfortunately, there were coaches who had not grasped the need for businesses to spotlight this particular competency. However, as the class progressed and as we each became more aware, we joined in one accord to model the way. Awareness creates key shifts in driving diversity as a business imperative.

Does it take a champion in a company to focus on diversity? We need business leaders who are advocates for diversity, especially at the executive level, so that conversations can continue for the executives who are still trying to figure it out, both for the organization and personally. Without champions, companies will not succeed in their diversity efforts.

In one hopeful trend, many companies have put in place specific performance measures related to diversity. Targets and specific numbers help bring focus to issues, in a way that numbers-driven people can understand.

Conscious and *intentional* leaders will become champions for diversity whether it is in their job description or they have numbers to meet. Each leader approaches the task in profound but often subtle ways. There are lessons to be learned and hopefully some of these leaders will one day tell their stories. Ira Hall, Ann Fudge, Darwin Davis Sr., Jesse Williams, Dr. Dorothy Height, Lloyd Trotter, John W. Thompson, and Linda Baker Keene are just a few names that come to mind. I am confident that stories of "struggles and detours to success" will be of benefit to those who follow.

THE FINAL THOUGHT . . . DIVERSITY

We must value and utilize all of the talent and resources that we can to improve the human condition and the viability and positive economic impact of business. How? We must *consciously* look for diverse talent to place on boards of directors, so that corporations can benefit from additional perspectives. Reach beyond the few, and find the many who can serve and make a difference. Mentor and share experiences to create learning opportunities meaningful enough to impact forever the way we live each day. Make a *conscious* and *intentional* effort to understand "generational diversity." The insight will strengthen your ability to communicate, leverage your ability to recruit and retain younger employees, and develop effective target marketing. Your benefit will be loyal customers for your business or organization.

When we prize Diversity, everybody wins!

DIVERSITY

LESSONS LEARNED (NUGGETS)

1 _____
2 _____
3 _____

CHECKLIST

☐ 1 Values diversity as a business imperative
☐ 2 Values diversity to strengthen human relationships
☐ 3 Constantly seeks to broaden awareness and experiences
☐ 4 Champions diversity
☐ 5 Creates diverse teams
☐ 6 Aware of blind spots and growth areas
☐ 7 Coaches diverse resources
☐ 8 Creates a diverse network
☐ 9 Comfortable flexing outside comfort zone
☐ 10 Promotes and respects diversity among employees
☐ 11 Maintains positive relationships with people at all levels
☐ 12 Welcomes culturally diverse experiences
___ *Total*

ACTIONS PLANNED   COMPLETION DATE

1 _____   _____
2 _____   _____
3 _____   _____
4 _____   _____
5 _____   _____

BARRIERS/BLIND SPOTS

1 _____
2 _____
3 _____

ACHIEVEMENTS

1 _____
2 _____
3 _____

To excel in performance, you need a plan that covers every facet of your life; it means self-ownership of your own power to determine your destiny. It is both qualitative and quantitative and measures your accomplishments and charts your progress as you achieve success. It is an essential component of the journey.

PERFORMANCE

Leaders have patience and perseverance of tinsel strength and are focused on reaching back and pulling others forward while continuing to succeed and achieve new heights.

CURTIS H. TEARTE
General Manager, IBM

The Boys Choir of Harlem and the Dance Theater of Harlem immediately come to mind when I think about models for consistent high quality and superb performance. I relish their work, whether it is a stirring solo, astounding harmonies, or the graceful poetics of dance. It is clear to me that to achieve the best possible performance requires practice. It takes patience and perseverance in order to achieve perfection.

I believe that when you do the work that you are meant to do on this earth, your life is work and your work is your life. It becomes your "life's work," and your daily mantra must be the consistent practice and development of the skills necessary to perform in an exceptional manner.

When it comes to performance, most people recognize that it is very important to have the best possible skills. But performance involves more than skills. It requires planning. You need a performance plan and a development plan. It doesn't matter whether you are a corporate executive, a fast-food restaurant manager, head of a community or service organization, an entrepreneur, a singer, a dancer, or a student. Having a plan helps you measure your accomplishments, chart your progress, and achieve extraordinary goals. What does your report card look like? Are your measures of success clearly documented? Do you have a plan to exceed your targets?

In the working world, the plan can provide for an equitable system of appraisal. Management can still alter or manipulate the parameters, like a teacher grading on a Bell curve, or make it competitive, like a race. However, if you are a proactive partner in the creation of the performance plan, if you are *conscious* and *intentional* about setting performance goals and objectives, even if the bar is set by someone else (board of directors, investors, or instructors), you have a vested interest in the successful outcome. This is especially true if your compensation (bonuses, stock options, salary increases, scholarships, and/or special awards) is connected to your performance. It is critical to understand how to leverage your earnings within the performance plan, particularly in a sales environment. Focus on defining the specific objectives, tasks, and activities that will drive the performance measures linked to your compensation.

It also is critical to understand the components of your plan, how they will be measured, and the expectations of the evaluator (your management, board of directors, teachers, etc.).

THE COACH APPROACH

Let's structure a performance plan (see chart on next page).

Keep in mind that in order to be successful in your performance, it is important to map your career interests to the work that you do. Sometimes that is not always possible. When you are thinking about your future career plans, however, it is worth considering.

What are the important elements of your plan? First, it should include a thorough description of all of your responsibilities. Next, include expectations (yours, the leader/manager's, board of director's, or a teacher's). There should be specific objectives. Each objective should have deadlines or time frames. Include how the objective will be measured and documented, such as achieving sales quotas, growth targets, profit and loss, and market share. Other key measures are

PERFORMANCE PLAN©

NAME:	Date of plan:
	Review date(s):

EVALUATOR:

RESPONSIBILITY 1.	RESPONSIBILITY 2.	RESPONSIBILITY 3.

OBJECTIVES (Specific, quantifiable, measurable)

❏	❏	❏
Measure:	Measure:	Measure:
Timeframe:	Timeframe:	Timeframe:
❏	❏	❏
Measure:	Measure:	Measure:
Timeframe:	Timeframe:	Timeframe:
❏	❏	❏
Measure:	Measure:	Measure:
Timeframe:	Timeframe:	Timeframe:

COMMENTS

OVERALL ASSESSMENT

Signature: _____	Date: _____
Evaluator Signature: _____	Date: _____
Second Line Signature: _____	Date: _____

© *Crystal Stairs, Inc. 2002*

customer satisfaction and the achievement of specific business targets. Winning new contracts for your business, raising a certain amount of money for your organization, or completing a specific project for school are other possible measures. Whether you do it on a weekly or monthly basis, it's important that you review your plan and truthfully assess where you are in relationship to your objectives.

At least once each quarter, provide a detailed update on the status of your performance to yourself, your management team or investors, your parents, etc. Make sure that you match your objectives with a list of specific accomplishments. Outline the objectives and projected accomplishments for the next ninety days. Solicit feedback from your evaluator about your performance to date and your ninety-day plans. Be clear about the appraisal system's measures as you go through those interim evaluation periods.

You also can solicit input from your peers, subordinates, or colleagues by using a 360° feedback process to give you another perspective on your work. An early wake-up call often will give you enough time to correct or focus on the area or areas in which you may be falling short of expectations. The Wonderlic Multi-Source Feedback Survey for Crystal Stairs Leadership Assets™ provides information from your selected circle of influence as to how well you are developing or have developed the 12 Leadership Assets™. Further information can be found in the reference section in Appendix B.

POTENTIAL 360° FEEDBACK RESPONDENTS

Manager

Client   Mentor

Project Team   ASSESSMENT   Team Leader
Members   REQUESTER

Subordinates   Peers

Direct Reports

One of the greatest benefits of successful performance can be the opportunity to take on new assignments or receive a promotion. New assignments are invigorating and provide an opportunity to learn new skills, work on new teams, and build your résumé. Use the coach approach as a way to view the opportunity: assess the expectations and what it will take to be successful, consider the possibilities, recognize what gaps must be bridged, acknowledge and plan to successfully navigate the learning period, and shift your style, behavior, and/or habits to adjust quickly to the new environment. View the planning process as an opportunity to focus on lifelong learning.

Excellent performers always find ways to break through. They create new paths. They exceed expectations because they create competitive advantages in everything they do. You must take your performance temperature. You must plot your journey. You set the bar.

MY STORY

From the beginning of my career, I always have made every effort to be prepared or to find ways to develop necessary skills or expertise. Early in my career, however, I had a manager who manipulated the quota system to assess my performance unfairly. It was a good lesson in understanding the system. What I learned was that quotas can be changed, depending upon whom the manager wants to make a hero. (Another opportunity to "manage transition.")

Later, when I had the opportunity to establish quotas for my own teams, I made sure that my driving forces were honesty, integrity, and fairness. I also made sure that I clearly communicated and articulated the challenges facing the team collectively as well as individually. There should be no surprises.

At the same time, it is important that you do not report inflated results to enhance your performance. At the end of the game, the truth will be revealed. A manager on my team once attempted to enhance his attainment by padding a customer's year-end order, without the sales rep's knowledge or the client's approval. To cover his tracks, he made it appear that a newer female sales rep on his team had handled the order. The young woman discovered the truth and told me. When the time was appropriate, I confronted him. Instead of taking responsibility, he blamed the woman. I was appalled that his personal value system not only permitted him to manipulate the quota system without any regrets, but also not tell the truth about it. Some people suffer from "truth aversion" disease.

The managers in these stories are not exceptions. They twisted the system for personal gain, yet both continue to advance their careers and still work for the corporation today. That's okay because we all continue to have lessons to learn. I can only trust that they learned the lessons and recovered from their illness.

One of the greatest lessons I ever learned was when I received an F in accounting during my first year in graduate school. Having received only A's and B's throughout my academic life, I was totally devastated. Eventually, I recognized that I had to take action. While completing an internship at R. J. Reynolds during the summer, I took a class at the University of North Carolina at Greensboro, which allowed the credit to be applied to my graduate work.

I could have viewed Professor Pekin Ogan, who flunked me in his course, as an adversary and a roadblock. Instead, his F became a moment of truth. I realized that I had to stretch myself. I needed to invest time to learn new fields of study to which I had not been exposed during college or in my life. I was trying to compete with students who had studied accounting for years and who went on to earn CPA degrees. I had to stop and assess my interests and my ability to achieve a level of performance that would dictate my future. Bridging this performance gap was the key to receiving my MBA. Thanks, Professor Ogan, for the lesson learned.

THE DEVELOPMENT PLAN

Your development plan should include areas in which you want and/or need to grow. Assessments provide a great starting point. How effective are you at working on a team? Do you need help with time management? Do you have all the skills you need to meet successfully the expectations of your performance plan? Complete a development plan on a periodic basis to continue focusing on your development and growth.

DEVELOPMENT PLAN©

NAME:		DATE:	

LEADERSHIP ASSET ASSESSMENT

STRONG	WORK IN PROGRESS	FOCUS
❑	❑	❑
❑	❑	❑
❑	❑	❑
❑	❑	❑
❑	❑	❑
❑	❑	❑

FOCUS

Leadership Asset	Development Actions Planned	Due Date
❑		
❑		
❑		

INTERESTS

Interests	Actions Planned	Due Date
❑		
❑		
❑		

ASPIRATIONS

Aspirations	Actions	By When
❑		
❑		
❑		

Skill Mentor	Relationship Mentor	Coach	

Personal Commitment Signature:		Date:

© *Crystal Stairs, Inc. 2002*

To help you achieve your developmental goals, think about establishing a skills-based mentoring relationship. A skills-based mentor can provide relevant information, model and transfer knowledge, and quickly bridge a skills gap. For example, I recall my first assignment as an executive assistant. Larry Sheffield had served in the position with the same executive prior to my appointment. Larry spent time with me explaining not only the skills necessary to be successful, but he also helped me to very quickly understand the operation of the office and the unique requirements of the executive. This skills-based mentoring allowed me to navigate the terrain quickly and to have a fast start in fulfilling the responsibilities.

Customers provide a finite benchmark for performance. They vote with the dollars they spend on your products and services. This tangible representation of performance is one that can quickly make or break you. It is one that provides an opportunity to assess your "truths." It is my belief that people still buy from people they like and from people with whom they have established relationships. The customer value proposition becomes a major grade on your report card that often will dictate the success of your performance.

Often managers "tolerate" performance issues. That is a disservice to employees because it shelters them from the knowledge that they need to bridge skill gaps. If either party abdicates the responsibility to laser inform or accept truth-saying, growth will stagnate.

COACHABLE MOMENT

I had a client who was given a new challenge at work. Although her manager thought she was ready for the additional responsibility, he told her it would be up to her to perform. As we talked about the new role, the first thing we determined was what she thought the end game would look like—what her ultimate objective was. Based on that, we developed the best approach to her new assignment. We could have created a plan that built upon her current skills and expertise and demonstrated to the team her ability to continue as a highly valued resource, but that would have been the easy road. She ultimately decided that her end game was to be known as an excellent leader with the discipline and competence to build a high-performance team by utilizing her expertise and battery of skills.

Harvey Coleman's book *Empowering Yourself* offers the thought-provoking perspective that performance is only ten percent of the game we play in corporate life. What's more, his documented work shows that the game has not changed for centuries. His formula for success—ten percent performance, thirty percent image, and sixty percent exposure (P.I.E.)—is a provocative approach to adopting performance as an entry ticket. He offers that individuals who want to fine-tune skills and move up in their profession must:

> ➤ *Perform* exceptionally well.
> ➤ Cultivate the proper *image*.
> ➤ Manage their *exposure* so the right people will know them.

Empowering Yourself is a must-read on the journey to developing your leadership assets. Performance is a critical success factor and we must find ways to exceed expectations while navigating the playing field.

In *JUMP-START Your Career: How the "STRENGTHS" that got you where you are today can hold you back tomorrow*, Dr. Lois Frankel offers an insightful perspective on why successful people fail, including:

> ➤ Overlooking the importance of people
> ➤ Inability to function effectively in a work group
> ➤ Failure to focus on image and communication
> ➤ Insensitivity to the reactions of others
> ➤ Difficulty working with authority
> ➤ Too broad or too narrow a vision
> ➤ Indifference to customer or client needs
> ➤ Working in isolation

THE FINAL THOUGHT . . . PERFORMANCE

Performance, as revealed by Harvey Coleman and Dr. Lois Frankel, is an expectation that often can elude and confuse those who believe it is the single most important factor dictating success in a job. Understanding the subtle yet profound views around this asset is key to success in your endeavors. Be willing to accept truth-saying. Be willing to seek answers to questions and take actions on areas revealed through assessments. It is only by passing the toughest tests that we are able to share testimonials on the other side. Performance is a fundamental asset that will indeed make or break us.

Find your life's work where the "j" in job is your joy. Then, excel in Performance!

PERFORMANCE

LESSONS LEARNED (NUGGETS)

1 _____
2 _____
3 _____

CHECKLIST

☐ 1 Excels in achieving performance targets and works hard to achieve goals
☐ 2 Clearly understands benchmarks for success
☐ 3 Documented performance plan with periodic reviews
☐ 4 Takes action to improve performance gaps
☐ 5 Constantly improves performance
☐ 6 Understands the "end game"
☐ 7 Establishes relationships with skills-based mentor
☐ 8 Keeps up to date on the latest technical developments that affect the job
☐ 9 Provides and accepts informal feedback regarding performance
☐ 10 Helps others achieve performance standards
☐ 11 Adapts effectively to changing job demands
☐ 12 Uses available resources to meet job demands
___ *Total*

ACTIONS PLANNED   COMPLETION DATE

1 _____   _____
2 _____   _____
3 _____   _____
4 _____   _____
5 _____   _____

BARRIERS/BLIND SPOTS

1 _____
2 _____
3 _____

ACHIEVEMENTS

1 _____
2 _____
3 _____

Break out of the mold of individualism and "me-ism" and share your expertise to resolve a challenge or accomplish a task. Leveraging a pool of talents and resources creates value for everyone. Know your role and how to flex best to serve the interest of the whole. Develop your personal and professional team.

TEAMWORK

Individuals can and do produce great work products. However, great teams produce superior work products and have fun doing so.

CARTER D. WOMACK
Executive Vice President, Value City Department Stores
Former International President of Phi Beta Sigma Fraternity Inc.
and the National Pan-Hellenic Council

When most of us were going to school, our teachers lauded individual performance, achievement, and success. If you were an ambitious kid, you took great pride in getting gold stars on your assignments, in having the best grades in class, in seeing your name listed on the honor roll, or in being inducted as a member of the National Honor Society. But when it came time for college and graduate school, you discovered a different situation. The word "team" became part of your lexicon. You were partnered with people, sometimes people you barely knew, to work on projects. Being a member of a collective body as opposed to doing work as an individual was both disconcerting and uncomfortable.

When you entered the business world, the word "team" took on a new meaning. You were expected not only to work with a group of people, usually co-workers, but also you often worked hard without getting any credit for your efforts. Many times, your team's success made your manager look great, and a promotion would be the reward. The other team members, however, were just faces in the crowd.

As a math major in college, my experience was very similar. I liked working alone, solving my own problems and equations. But in graduate school it became very clear to me that to survive and succeed in the culture at Indiana University, I needed networking and teamwork skills in addition to my book knowledge and intellectual capabilities. I had always used my ability to study hard and earn exceptional grades to hide the fact that I was an introvert and preferred to work alone. I needed to make a change in my attitude. To be successful when I graduated, I needed to learn more than the lessons being taught in the classroom. The culture of Indiana University foreshadowed the corporate world to which my MBA would open doors. It was imperative that I learn how to work within teams.

I switched my major from finance to marketing. I pushed myself to work on case-study teams and to participate in group projects. I learned to pay close attention to detail and listen to what people said *without* words. I learned how to work with people who had different beliefs and perspectives. I learned what it meant to be a responsible team member. I learned to be flexible, how to change directions quickly, how to conserve and manage time.

When I joined IBM, I discovered that even if I had skills—technical support, marketing, sales, or administration—I was expected to work on teams in order to deliver products or solutions for a client. Enhancing my teamwork skills became an imperative for me.

We often have blind spots associated with being members of a team. We wonder how we can contribute, whether we will be understood. We're concerned about how our performance will be measured and whether we will receive any recognition for our efforts. The challenge, however, is developing a team-oriented consciousness. I believe teamwork is critical in order to leverage the best possible talent to resolve a problem or accomplish a task. The more expertise shared, the more viable the solution.

TEAM ROLES

I developed a greater appreciation of team dynamics through Inscape Publishing's "Innovate with C.A.R.E." training program. Like behavior styles, certain roles invariably emerge in teams. While those roles change, depending upon the team, they nonetheless continue to exist. The five roles are Creator, Advancer, Refiner, Executor, and Facilitator.

Think about these five roles for a moment. "Team Crystal" has been mobilized to roll out a new product that will provide innovation in the marketplace. The team is responsible for developing every facet of the campaign. Someone has to *create* what the campaign will be and develop the rationale for it. Another member has to recognize the ideas that have the most potential and promote or *advance* them. The team needs another person who is analytical and orderly, the person who is always asking the tough questions to see whether there are any flaws in the plans so that they can be *refined*. Another team member takes responsibility for making sure that, once all of the ideas are gathered and refined, a plan is drawn up that includes time frames, objectives, and measurements so that the plan can be *executed*. Of course, when you bring together in one room such a diverse group of team members, who motivates them to work together? There has to be someone who *facilitates* the meeting and keeps things running smoothly.

High-performance teams recognize all of the roles and flex in and out of the roles depending on the needs of the team. Look at your team and analyze which roles the different members are playing. If a role is missing, it is a disadvantage for your team. Do you have a tendency to perform a certain role? Do you have a preference for a particular role? One critical point: You don't always have to play the same role on every team. As a matter of fact, in order to grow and develop, you should strive to learn all the roles and perform them when necessary.

The distinctions often remind me of a basketball game. The point guard, for example, is the *facilitator*, who directs the flow of the play. The power forward *advances* the offense (and leads the defense). The small forward, working on the wing, helps *refine* the play and is available for a three-point shot if the point guard passes the ball. The shooting guard, working the other wing or playing in the lane, helps *create* new plays if the other team's defense forces a change in plans. And the center is in the lane or underneath the basket to *execute* on the fast break or block a shot. Star players also compete against each other and then play together when East plays West during the All-Star Game. Or they respond to a higher calling when together they compete as representatives of their country at the Olympics.

Does behavior come into play? The answer is yes. But don't confuse behavior style with team roles. Not all *C* (*conscientiousness*) behavior styles, for example, make great executors or facilitators. You have to look at the bigger picture. Behavior styles potentially can overwhelm a team. That's why the role of the facilitator is key. Some behavior styles want a written meeting agenda so that they can see the tasks at hand. More people-oriented styles—*I* (*influence*) and *S* (*steadiness*)—will go with the flow and create as they go. Understanding how people interact will determine how they engage.

LEVERAGING TEAM INTERACTION

It is also important to note that there are key distinctions between the following types of team interactions: competitive, cooperative, and collaborative. Why do I think it is important to understand these distinctions? As business models emerge in which alliances, partnerships, mergers, and acquisitions provide new approaches to business opportunities, it is important to be able to interact appropriately in any of these models and to leverage them to achieve new possibilities.

With coaching as an example, the opportunities are too abundant and the services too broadly needed by clients to be concerned with competitive jockeying. Relationships often are established based on reputation, trust, and expertise. Clients will be attracted to you when you deliver results. Time spent competing is time wasted. However, be positioned to win with references, a unique value proposition, and a history of integrity and values. These traits set businesses apart. You will be prepared to compete.

On occasion, a coach is asked to cooperate with another coach in a cooperative spirit. This is a model of "give and take" for a specific transaction. The need to work together is clear and agendas should be put aside to meet the client's objectives. When the objective has been achieved, measure the results in terms of the client's satisfaction level and the level to which each party benefited.

Collaborative interaction takes on a behavior where win-win becomes the key measure of success. The end goal can be accomplished only through working together with the faith and trust that the sum total is greater than any of its pieces. Collaborative opportunities require a strong foundation of behavior and values that allows the win-win to emerge for all parties.

On a recent engagement, I subcontracted two other trainers to work with me in coaching clients during an outplacement opportunity. Individually, I would not have been able to service the clients. In responding to my clients' request, none of us would have been as strong as all of us together. By joining our strengths, however, we built a partnership that has evolved into a new offering, a collaborative service each of our firms can use to win contracts.

THE TEAM CHARTER

Set parameters for success from the beginning, such as defining "what the win looks like" at the end of the process. Make sure everyone understands the team's vision, its goals and objectives, and the way the plan will be executed. If everyone is clear on his or her role, you can build a high-performance team with strong relationships that will benefit all of its members. The entire team's performance will move to the next level because of the team's strengths and dynamics.

Let's consider the distinction between a high-performance team and a work group. Work groups don't *consciously* and *intentionally* build parameters around how the deliverable will look. Their approach is simply to execute the task, with or without one another. They don't agree to disagree. They lock on their differences and don't move forward. Would you prefer to be assigned to a work group or contribute to a high-performance team?

Diversity is a critical component of a high-performance team. I refer not just to cultural diversity, but to diversity of thought, experience, and expertise as well. If you are pulling together a team that will work internationally, you might also want to take into consideration cultural differences, expectations, operational procedures, and the way day-to-day cultural nuances come into play.

Partnering with international team members is an opportunity to learn more about the global economy. Given the advent of a business model that is Internet-based, the possibilities and opportunities are much broader. Preparing to be a contributing member with international expertise that will broaden your business opportunities is a major skill that will serve you well.

TEAM COMMUNICATION AND CELEBRATION

High-performance teams understand all the dynamics of team interaction, including how individuals communicate, receive messages, and manage the interaction. A team's communication skills—how well they communicate with each other and understand each other's behavior styles—can dictate the success or failure of a project. When teams are performing at their peak, people are flexing in and out of their styles and are working together to achieve common objectives and goals.

A high-performance team defines roles that encourage each member to step up to the plate and deliver a hit. The Coach Approach allows the team to be assessed at any given time so that the gaps can be determined and a strategy can be developed to build the bridge. The team must be facilitated in a manner that strengthens it so that it can successfully achieve its objectives.

High-performance teams also know how and when to celebrate. They celebrate the stages of their success, rather than waiting until the end to share their good positive experiences. Celebration is a requisite part of the team dynamic. It is the distinction between a high-performance team and a work group.

Planning the seventy-fifth Anniversary for Zeta Phi Beta in 1995 represented the ultimate in high-performance teamwork. During the initial planning session, we envisioned a historical celebration, deplete of distractions and filled with memorable moments. The year-long celebration was carefully developed; each member was assigned specific tasks and activities as a part of the total plan. Additional resources were recruited or hired to partner with the team. Through the master facilitator, our conference planning chairperson, Doris McAdams Stokes, the event proved to be a great success because each team member executed her role flawlessly. The events were professional and classy and left attendees with memories that will last a lifetime.

On the night before I departed from our major event in Washington, D.C., we celebrated in a way that created special memories for me. Vercilla Brown, the executive director; Vickie Robinson, the deputy executive director; and Kim Sawyer, my special assistant, surprised me by renting a fully equipped minibus. We had dinner at a wonderful restaurant and toured the city of Washington, D.C., at night. We ran up the steps of the Lincoln Memorial, and, as we breathed a deep sigh of relief, I knew it was a breath of life I would never forget. Ladies . . . *thanks . . .* job well done!

THE COACH APPROACH

Cynder Niemela and Rachael Lewis authored the book *Leading High Impact Teams: The Coach Approach to Peak Performance.* Together, with more than four decades of experience, they developed "The Top 10 High Impact Team Practices." These practices offer a framework for coaching, leading, or actively engaging the work of a team. I believe in the statement offered by Cynder and Rachael that "When the team leader and team members intentionally commit themselves to strive for excellence as they define it, they make a crucial investment in their team's long-term success." Are you committed?

THE TOP 10 HIGH IMPACT TEAM PRACTICES©	
PRACTICE	DESCRIPTION
1 Shared Purpose and Vision	❑ If you asked each of us why we are here as a team and what we're working towards, the answer would be the same and you can see it in our
2 Shared Leadership	❑ We each take responsibility for the team being successful. Leadership is propagated throughout the team: all members operate with the same purpose and vision as the leader.
3 Measurable Performance Targets and Definable Goals	❑ We have agreed to specific, measurable, achievable, and time bound goals; they include both business and team development objectives. ❑ We have established and we track measurable performance targets that move us towards our goals. We regularly evaluate how we are working together as a high impact team.
4 Clear Roles and Responsibilities	❑ We each know not only the activities we are individually accountable for, but also what we are collectively responsible to produce. Each team member's role is clear. ❑ We respect each person's role and openly discuss our expectations for the responsibilities of each role.

continued . . .

PRACTICE	DESCRIPTION
5 Active Sponsorship	❏ Our sponsors are involved and committed to our success, and support us in clearing away obstacles. Our sponsors are proponents of our work and delegate the appropriate authority. ❏ We have the resources we need to be successful: information, money, time, space, and talent.
6 Effective Team Process	❏ We have a working agreement for our approach to our work and revise it when necessary. ❏ We have practices for effective meetings, integrating new team members, decision making, and problem solving.
7 Enhanced Team Competency	❏ Our team acknowledges conflict and deals with it when it arises. ❏ We have the flexibility to integrate change. ❏ We are able to correct our course when off course, and adapt to changing conditions.
8 Synergistic Collaboration and Innovation	❏ Trust, accountability, and integrity are strong in our relationships. Communication and dialogue foster action. ❏ We collaborate to innovate new products or services and to solve problems when they arise. ❏ We use both task and task-free activities to infuse our team with creativity, celebration, and renewal.
9 Meaningful Recognition and Rewards	❏ We are committed to each other's and the team's success. We acknowledge both individual and team achievements and personal development. ❏ We recognize values-based performance in a meaningful way.
10 Quality Relationships with Stakeholders and Other Teams	❏ We coordinate our efforts with other stakeholders in a timely fashion. ❏ We develop good relationships with other teams. ❏ Our work is integrated with the company's overall business goals.

© High Impact Publishing, 2001

As you continue to strengthen your leadership assets related to team-work, review "The High Impact Team Assessment" offered in Cynder and Rachael's book. It provides a framework to initiate, monitor, and measure the effectiveness of the team. Focus on implementing these practices and utilizing the assessment to build strong, "high impact" teams.

COACHABLE MOMENTS

I was assigned to a reengineering team at IBM. We were charged with exploring and recommending a new supply-chain management system that would be implemented worldwide across multiple divisions. About thirty people from twenty or more countries, divisions, and/or backgrounds were assigned to the team. Our charge was multidimensional. First, we had to understand how to work with one another and to communicate in a common language. Second, we had to develop parameters for the project and a plan. Third, we had to execute the plan and make sure the system would result in tremendous financial benefit to the company.

This was my first international project for the company. I remember wondering what role I would serve and how I would work in the subgroups that were set up to break the project into smaller, workable components. Initially, I was uncomfortable. I recalled my first reaction to working on case-study teams while in graduate school. I was the observer on the team. My opinion had to be pulled out of me. I tended to dwell on the details and on assessing other people's opinions. Now I understand how my behavior style came into play.

Initially, I saw myself in the same role on the IBM team. This time, though, I was given much more responsibility. The assignment required that I travel to Italy to analyze the supply chain system and to interview company executives. We needed a plan that associates across the world would support. I was truly out of my comfort zone. When I walked through the streets of Italy and even through the halls of IBM Italy, the stares alone were uncomfortable. Adapting to customs while faced with specific tasks that needed to be accomplished also was a very challenging, learning opportunity. Upon our return home, the team assembled the story of global supply-chain management across IBM. It was an experience that provided many lessons. But for the first time, I understood the far-reaching implications of having a highly functional, high-performance team whose strength was its diversity of opinion, expertise, and experience.   Barbara Ellis —Thanks!

In our personal lives, we often find ourselves serving on different types of teams: as an elected or appointed officer in an organization, as the leader of a community initiative, as planner for the family vacation, or as part of a major multiorganizational campus service project. We even find it necessary to build teams when we are job-searching, looking for people to help with a project, or when we want to organize a weekend gathering.

Team 100™ is an exercise I recommend as a way to build networks and develop your personal team. Take the time to think through your "TEAM," and start to nurture and develop the critical relationships. Information on obtaining the "Team 100™" Assessment is provided in Appendix B.

I also recommend adding "Love 25" as a final step in building the team. "Love 25" represents twenty-five members of your team who add particular value to your life's journey. Develop mechanisms to stay in touch with them regularly.

A FINAL THOUGHT . . . TEAMWORK

Teamwork concepts can be applied to any situation in which you work with one or more individuals with the goal of working to achieve a mutually beneficial outcome. We are only as strong as our high-performance teams, and each successful effort provides energy and encouragement for all of the team members.

Exercise your Teamwork!

TEAMWORK

LESSONS LEARNED (NUGGETS)
1 _____
2 _____
3 _____

CHECKLIST
☐ 1   Aware of team roles
☐ 2   Understands and executes required personal roles
☐ 3   Strives to achieve consistent team effectiveness
☐ 4   Engages team communication
☐ 5   Active and contributing participant on the team
☐ 6   Flexes behavior to benefit the team
☐ 7   Creates high-performance teams
☐ 8   Makes distinction between compete, cooperate, and collaborate
☐ 9   Earns a reputation of trust and dependability
☐ 10   Creates win-win scenarios
☐ 11   Delivers significant contributions to the team
☐ 12   Celebrates milestones as a team
___ *Total*

ACTIONS PLANNED   COMPLETION DATE
1 _____   _____
2 _____   _____
3 _____   _____
4 _____   _____
5 _____   _____

BARRIERS/BLIND SPOTS
1 _____
2 _____
3 _____

ACHIEVEMENTS
1 _____
2 _____
3 _____

The integral role that technology plays in your life and your work mandates understanding how to utilize it both as an information provider and productivity tool. The demands of new generations are rapidly dictating the quick pace of change in the world of technology. Those interactions are providing access and choices as never before experienced in history.

TECHNOLOGY

Throughout history, the victories have gone to those who have embraced technological change and used these advances to improve their circumstances. Those who have not understood the importance of technology have left the victors to write their history.

R. STEVE EDMONSON
Vice President, Cardinal Health, Inc.;
Chairperson, Information Technology Senior Management Forum (ITSMF)

Technology literacy is one of the essential tools in every leader's tool kit. A firm understanding of the impact of technology to both our business and personal roles changes our perspective and the way we respond to issues that impact our various constituencies. These skills are so important that sometimes they make the difference between effectiveness and ineffectiveness in the various roles that we play.

BRUCE C. CARVER
Chief Information Officer, Quaker Foods and Beverages

One of the greatest revolutions of the twentieth century was technological advancement. Each gain irrevocably altered every facet of American life. Within the short period of fifty years, for example, telephones went from land lines to cellular. Music went from being recorded on long-playing albums (LPs), containing twelve or fifteen songs on two sides, to digital discs that have the capacity to store more than one thousand songs. Carbon paper gave way to photocopy machines. Typewriters were replaced by computers. Instead of using bank tellers, more of us are using automated teller machines (ATMs) or are banking online. Lecture halls no longer are the only learning environments for students; today they can learn in virtual classrooms, with classmates from anywhere in the world. And let's not forget the virtual office. You are more likely to carry your office in a laptop tucked inside a computer carrying case on wheels than to spend your time seated at a desk or cubicle, looking out of the window.

What looked like a futuristic life of robots, talking computers, and space-station living was depicted by the syndicated cartoon *The Jetsons*, which first aired in the early 1960s. Today, it looks more like our reality. I cringe to think of what concepts in this book, particularly in this chapter, quickly will become antiquated. As a result, I hope to provide a framework for technology as a Leadership Asset™ and reasons why it is important to keep it at the forefront of your lifelong learning plan.

The general public's access to the Internet has made technology the number-one vehicle to information. It is, therefore, critically important that we proactively use and expose individuals to this tool and become students of technology. Because of the integral role that technology plays in our lives and our work, the key is to understand how to utilize it both as an information provider and as a productivity tool.

A personal technology curriculum can be created in a number of ways. Schools and libraries often offer classes in addition to providing access to a system. Computer retail stores often have classes for a fee on specific topics. I actually bought a CompUSA® membership and took classes for six months just to be exposed to new applications and to become more proficient in some with which I had "tinkered" for many years. Community colleges also provide excellent opportunities to develop computer and application skills.

The advent of "e-learning" has opened the door for advanced education via Internet universities. My personal experience with Corporate Coach University International (CCUI) has helped me understand that the possibilities of alternative learning approaches are infinite and phenomenal. The reach is unparalleled. The future offers great promise for global education through technology.

MY STORY

My first introduction to technology was in 1976, as a fellow in the Consortium for Graduate Study in Business Program at Indiana University. I had to use a card-punch machine for class in the university's computer lab. I was in my element. With my math background and the power of that keypunch machine, I could program Cobol with the best of them. I loved the logic and the challenge. My *C* behavior was in details heaven.

In 1981, I purchased my first PC. An early entrant to the world of home computing, I paid five thousand dollars for my first computer and made two monthly payments through the IBM credit union. It was an expensive toy, but to me it was more fascinating than driving a new car.

The machine was powerful. It had sixty-four megabytes (MB) of memory, a great little dial-in modem, and a hard drive that was about two MB. I remember reading the DOS manual and learning to manipulate files and commands to make the system perform functions. I learned VisiCalc™ and EasyWriter™. What great products! I was able to type reports and change them on the computer and even do calculations with formulas that the computer remembered for me. I became a zealot for technology learning and experimentation.

I'm finding it hard to recall what only twenty years ago was the foundation for a major shift in the way we live and work. Given the capability of systems today and the immediate access to information, it seems like another lifetime. Because of the speed of change and its far-reaching impact, I believe technology is a critical asset because it is the backbone of the way most businesses operate today and how people will learn. Technology enhances both professional and personal productivity.

COACHABLE MOMENTS

When dealing with technology, coachable moments are ongoing. Be sensitive to the potential for the communications overload that technology can cause. Use technology that makes YOU productive. For example, you don't need the latest model of a car to travel between your home and your office. As long as you can get from point A to point B, the car serves its purpose. When it starts to break down, or is costing more to repair than it is worth, then you need to make choices and decisions about whether to replace it. The same holds true for technology. You don't *need* a new PC every year, unless there is a need to change parameters: memory, applications, speed, or an enhanced need for security. You can't afford to respond to the rapid-fire changes in technology just for the sake of technology.

Given the proliferation of technology tools, you can spend a lot of time evaluating the bells and whistles. The trade-off is the value of time in making an immediate choice and moving forward or getting bogged down in *C*-behavior until you get it exactly right. The life cycle of technology is such that you can always be confident that a faster or better system is right around the corner. Make decisions based on the best knowledge at hand with a solution that meets your requirements, and move forward.

COACH APPROACH

The Coach Approach to technology is one of continuous learning. Look at the following Technology Checklist© as a method to think through where you are and use technology as an asset.

TEN POINT TECHNOLOGY CHECKLIST©

1. GENERAL QUESTIONS
- ❑ How will I work and live?
- ❑ Where will I perform the work?
- ❑ How will I use technology?
- ❑ Who else will use the technology?
- ❑ How do I prefer to do business?
- ❑ When and how to communicate?
- ❑ What price for productivity?
- ❑ How much do I spend?
- ❑ What are my technology phobias?
- ❑ Application residence?
- ❑ Where is the best place to buy?
- ❑ What applications are integrated?
- ❑ Can the technology be updated?
- ❑ Company's core competency?
- ❑ How much data do I need to store?
- ❑ Consolidate information?
- ❑ Tech priorities?
- ❑ Impact of technology on career?
- ❑ Impact on my life?
- ❑ Others _____

2. NEEDS/WANTS ASSESSMENT
- ❑ Communication
- ❑ Run business
- ❑ Type of site
- ❑ Commerce enabled
- ❑ Family history
- ❑ Photo collection
- ❑ Online or offline
- ❑ Anytime, anyplace, anywhere?
- ❑ International requirements
- ❑ Others _____

3. FINANCIALS
- ❑ Price comparison
- ❑ Where to buy
- ❑ Do it yourself or outsource
- ❑ Pricing
  - ❑ One of a kind
  - ❑ Custom
  - ❑ Off the shelf
- ❑ How to buy

- ❑ Budget
- ❑ Others _____

4. APPLIANCES
- ❑ Computer
  - ❑ Desktop
  - ❑ Laptop
  - ❑ Handheld
  - ❑ PDA
  - ❑ Email
  - ❑ Camera
  - ❑ Keyboard
  - ❑ Applications
  - ❑ Others _____
  - ❑ Web TV
- ❑ Server
- ❑ Router
- ❑ Network
- ❑ Printer—laser, inkjet, photo
- ❑ Digital—camera, video, music, voice, notes
- ❑ Fax
- ❑ Copier
- ❑ Scanner (handheld)
- ❑ Multifunction machines
- ❑ Phone
- ❑ Pager
- ❑ Data storage
- ❑ Memory
- ❑ UPS
- ❑ Surge protection
- ❑ Radio
- ❑ Others _____

5. ACCESSORIES
- ❑ Ribbons/cartridges
- ❑ Paper
- ❑ Memory
- ❑ Storage
- ❑ Keyboards (PDA)
- ❑ Surge Protector/UPS
- ❑ Connectivity
- ❑ Electronic wallet
- ❑ Monitors
- ❑ Smart home
- ❑ Card scan
- ❑ Others _____

6. APPLICATIONS
- ❑ Email
- ❑ Instant pessaging
- ❑ Word processing
- ❑ Spreadsheet
- ❑ Organization
- ❑ Database
- ❑ Graphics
- ❑ Presentations
- ❑ Home management
- ❑ Client management
- ❑ Personal finances
- ❑ Online investing
- ❑ Online banking
- ❑ Online meetings
- ❑ Accounting
- ❑ Global tracking/directions
- ❑ Travel arrangements
- ❑ Shopping/selling
- ❑ Auctions
- ❑ Price comparison
- ❑ Note taking
- ❑ Kids
- ❑ Education
- ❑ Greeting cards
- ❑ Publish
- ❑ E-book
- ❑ Communication
- ❑ Research
- ❑ Get a job
- ❑ Find a home
- ❑ Music
- ❑ Others _____

7. RESPONSIBILITY
- ❑ Family
- ❑ Associations
- ❑ Organizations
- ❑ Schools/centers
- ❑ Girls and tech
- ❑ Work donations
- ❑ Math and science
- ❑ Mentor/volunteer
- ❑ Challenged
- ❑ Elders
- ❑ Give tech gifts
- ❑ Others _____

continued ...

8. EDUCATION
- ❏ Classroom
- ❏ Internet-based
- ❏ CD ROM
- ❏ Virtual MBA
- ❏ Conferences
- ❏ Trade shows
- ❏ Network/chats
- ❏ Books/magazines
- ❏ Newspapers
- ❏ Others _____

9. SERVICES
- ❏ System MA/Help
- ❏ Software MA/Help
- ❏ Internet service provider
  - ❏ Space
  - ❏ Monthly fees
  - ❏ 24/7
  - ❏ Offerings
- ❏ Domain registration
- ❏ Email address

- ❏ Advertising
- ❏ Commerce enable
- ❏ Innovation
- ❏ Others _____

10. CRYSTAL STAIRS TENETS
- ❏ Build your foundation
  - ❏ Personal email
  - ❏ Domain name
- ❏ Budget and invest in tech
- ❏ Develop a tech plan
  - ❏ Business
  - ❏ Personal
  - ❏ Family
- ❏ Commit to lifelong learning
- ❏ Go scouting and surfing
- ❏ Bookmark the learning
- ❏ Dedicate time
- ❏ Backup your data
- ❏ Learn the language
- ❏ Complete five-step action plan

NUGGETS:
1.
2.
3.

CHALLENGES:
1.
2.
3.

GOAL:

ACTION	By when	CONTACTS	Date comp.
1.			
2.			
3.			
4.			
5.			

© Crystal Stairs, Inc. 2000

Companies should continue to be vigilant about upgrading technology services so that their information and/or products are easily accessible to their customers, any time or any place. In a *New York Times* advertisement in January 2002, IBM promoted its e-business solutions as the newest utility (joining gas, water, and electricity) and inferred how information technology has now become part of society's lifeline. Cutting-edge organizations offer technology-based training to educate their clients and associates about their products and services.

Nonprofit organizations, such as the United Negro College Fund (UNCF), have integrated the need for technological advancement as a component of their fundraising activities for historically black colleges and universities. That strategy opens the doors for both philanthropists and foundations to donate equipment or other technology resources. I applaud both Microsoft and the UNCF for the partnerships they have established in the area of technology and scholarships.

BRIDGING THE DIGITAL DIVIDE

There is a community of technologically astute individuals who have a responsibility to bridge the gap between the "technology haves" and the "technology have-nots." That gap is called the digital divide. How do we shift from a digital divide society to a digital provide society? Those of us who have the knowledge, understanding, and resources to bring technology to individuals, organizations, and businesses that do not have it have the responsibility to get involved. Organizations such as the Black Data Processing Association (BDPA) and the Information Technology Senior Management Forum (ITSMF) are working to bridge the gap. They are trying to make sure there is a pipeline for resources, information, jobs, and knowledge between those in business and those seeking access. Their efforts are making a difference.

Providing broad access to technology necessitates our reaching back and executing the principle of "each one, teach one" by forging partnerships between grass-roots initiatives and corporate outreach strategies. The Black Family Technology Awareness Week is an example. Sponsored by Career Communications Group and IBM, the campaign encourages blacks to incorporate technology into their daily lives. This model alliance, founded by Tyrone Taborn of Career Communications

Groups, reaches out to the community through essay contests in which students compete to win computers for both school and home, as well as church sponsorships of "High-tech Sunday" and "Family-tech" nights. Black technologists in the community are working to expand the "technology" network, and their success should be applauded.

THE NEXT GENERATION

We live in a technology-driven, network-wired, virtual-learning world. For future generations, hand-held computers will be considered the price to enter the game, simply another check-off on the school supply list. Making an investment in technology today will pay significant dividends in the future. Think of giving technology-related tools as gifts to charitable organizations or to members of your family—especially your children. Even video games can have a positive effect. In addition to the development of hand/eye coordination skills, video games are causing shifts in the way we use technology as a means of education. Games that teach job skills or challenge children to think are excellent training tools.

Children are great case studies of technology usage because they are fearless and phobia-free. They learn by pushing buttons to see what happens. I am learning a lot from my child. Exposed to computers at school and spending time on her own laptop, she is teaching me techniques and tips that are boosting my productivity. A computer always has been part of her environment. It is her toy and her education tool as well; it plays music, screens films, does research for homework, provides presentations and graphics for projects. Essentially, it has replaced the television, record player, and movie theater of my generation. What will the world look like for *her* children?

Recently, her school asked for my email address. I suppose it beats photocopying papers for several hundred students, papers that end up being discarded. I wonder how much money the school will save by using email to communicate with parents. I wonder if all the parents have access to email at home. Anyway, it certainly will be a step toward a more environmentally conscious world!

A FINAL THOUGHT . . . TECHNOLOGY

We must not let technology replace the need for personal contact and interaction, something to which we must all be *consciously* and *intentionally* attuned. Although it may seem more productive to send an email or leave a voice mail when you feel as if you don't "have time" to talk, nothing can adequately replace person-to-person dialogue. Use technology to "make time," rather than using it to "save time." Integrate its use in your life so that you can maintain necessary personal connections in what could become an impersonal, disconnected world.

Surf the waves of Technology!

TECHNOLOGY

LESSONS LEARNED (NUGGETS)

1 _____
2 _____
3 _____

CHECKLIST

☐ 1 Integrates technology for personal productivity
☐ 2 Uses technology to increase work performance
☐ 3 Periodically reviews the "Technology Checklist"
☐ 4 Continuously learning/using new technology
☐ 5 Intentional technology investment plan
☐ 6 Uses e-learning to explore new possibilities
☐ 7 Consciously balances human interaction with technology ease
☐ 8 Seeks ways to bridge the technology "access" gap
☐ 9 Adapts effectively to changing technology
☐ 10 Provides support to technology advancement at academic institutions
☐ 11 Ensures access within our families and extended community
☐ 12 Automates personal tasks that provide greater work/life equation choice

___ *Total*

ACTIONS PLANNED   COMPLETION DATE

1 _____   _____
2 _____   _____
3 _____   _____
4 _____   _____
5 _____   _____

BARRIERS/BLIND SPOTS

1 _____
2 _____
3 _____

ACHIEVEMENTS

1 _____
2 _____
3 _____

One of the greatest skills of a *conscious* and *intentional* leader is the ability to govern the use of time. Time governance is self-management, the acquiring and implementation of good habits, priority setting, and sensitivity to others' time expectations.

TIME MANAGEMENT

I have only just a minute,
Only sixty seconds in it
Forced upon me, can't refuse it,
Didn't seek it, didn't choose it
But it's up to me to use it
I must suffer if I lose it
Give account if I abuse it
Just a tiny little minute
But an eternity is in it!

DR. BENJAMIN MAYS
From *Quotable Quotes*

No matter how many meetings, deadlines, telephone calls, or family obligations we have on a daily basis, there still are only twenty-four hours in each day. Sometimes it seems impossible to manage it all.

One of the greatest skills of a *conscious* and *intentional* leader is the ability to maximize the use of time. Time management is more than plotting your life out on calendars and to-do lists. It is self-management. It is the mastery of good habits that require you to set and stick to priorities.

The greatest benefit of mastering time is gaining control over your legacy. What do I mean by that? People will remember you for the great work you've done, for the wonderful things you've accomplished, not for what you *said* you would do and didn't accomplish. (Or maybe they will.) It is important to master your time so that you can achieve the goals that will represent your life's legacy.

At one point in my life, I had lots of balls in the air. In training sessions and seminars, I often am asked how I made it all work. As a mother, a vice president, an international president, and several other titles, I myself sometimes wondered how it all got completed. I respond with two tips: Create a network of supporters and do what's most important. I think I learned this skill from the many women who were my role models. One I would single out is Lullelia Walker Harrison, the first executive director for Zeta Phi Beta and the twelfth international president. She did it all. Her energy was contagious, and her focus was piercing. She is a great woman, a great leader, and a great time manager.

THE COACH APPROACH

What matters most to you? If you were to make a list of all the things you need to accomplish today, what would be on it? Make that list now. Be sure to include *everything*, even those things you want to do but lack the time, or so you think, to do them. Review your list.

One of the principles outlined by author Stephen Covey in *The 7 Habits of Highly Effective People* is "Begin with the end in mind." It means you start each day, each project, each activity with the knowledge of what you will accomplish. To manage and master time, you must have a sense of purpose and direction. Going back to your list, write down the projected end result of each of your tasks or activities.

Review your list again. Of all of the things you wrote down, what is the most important task or activity that you must accomplish *today*? What is second? Third? Is there anything that can be pushed to tomorrow or the next day? How long do you estimate each of these tasks or activities will take? How many hours do you intend to work today?

NAVIGATING THE MAZE

Think about all of the processes you just used to compile this list: adjusting attitude, setting goals, prioritizing, analyzing, planning, and scheduling. The management of time requires the mastery of a process of steps in order to achieve your goals and objectives.

The more specific we are about what we must accomplish, the more we begin to focus on making it happen. Bob LaBant calls it "maniacal focus." I'm not suggesting that you maniacally plan your time. I'm urging you to make every effort to be present in everything that you do; make every effort to be *focused* on the task.

Time management also is a skill we can use to integrate the Leadership Assets™ into our daily lives. By using time to ensure we are *consciously* and *intentionally* following through on our goals and objectives, we can meet or exceed our targets.

Beware of what we refer to in coaching as *tolerations.* A toleration is something to which we give time that we otherwise would invest in achieving a priority. In time management, a toleration is a time robber. It is important that you don't tolerate the theft of your time by engaging in nonpriority activities and tasks. Learn to incorporate "no" into your vocabulary.

I am not a person who accepts tardiness with a welcoming, calm attitude. It is a trigger that can set me off into a behavior "no-fly" zone. Individuals with *I* behavior who call to chit-chat or who want to just "do lunch" also are tolerations in my work/life. I struggle not to offend but to protect the space that I have carved to manage my equation. The drive and *D* behavior that reveals itself when "time is money" or a trade-off in my self-care time, weighs heavy on the equation. Certainly, being conscientious about the value of my services as represented by billable time is the *C* inherent in my behavior. It can often unconsciously introduce the wrong behavior when I start drilling toward the mission.

I also think it is important to understand time management by using the paradigm of competition, cooperation, and collaboration. Allocate your time based on the approach that you think will produce the desired results. Don't tolerate interruptions; they impact the time you've scheduled to work or focus on a goal.

TIME MANAGEMENT TOOLS

Writing lists on scraps of paper is not time management. At the very least, you need a notebook. A calendar would be better. Whatever tool you choose, remember that it must be something that will fit your lifestyle. It should be simple to use and help you make the best of each day.

Some people use PC-based calendar systems, electronic organizers, or other tools. If you decide to go electronic, make sure you back up the data on your PC. Because it is both a source of time management and a repository of critical information, it is important to ensure that it is secure. I once had a "Wizard" stolen from my hotel room, and I lost a Palm Pilot on an airplane. What I learned is that losing this valuable resource (which was not backed up) was like having time stolen from me, time I could have spent in a meeting, networking, or with a loved one. Taking the extra precaution to safeguard your important data on electronic equipment can be a lifesaver down the line.

Managing paperwork is another very important component of time management. Schedule time both to check and immediately respond to email and other types of correspondence. Allow time to straighten your desk and file important papers. Even if you work well in a messy environment, time spent searching for a piece of paper that you need is time wasted.

Think about coaching as a time-management tool, too. It forces discipline in your life. My first coach, Donna Coulson, coached me to understand that as a person with high *DC* behavior, I was very task-oriented and did not spend enough time focusing on myself. Her coaching focused on making extreme self-care a necessary component of my life. We worked on managing time through my calendar to allow me to build in sacred personal time. More than time for pampering myself, it is time preserved for personal development and growth. Build in personal time on your calendar, and hold firm to it to rejuvenate your spirit and soul.

The thirty minutes to an hour spent weekly with a coach, assessing where you are with your objectives, can be a constant reminder of the value of taking care of yourself. After all, it helps you maintain the energy required to produce results. It is a period of serious focus that helps you determine the most productive use of your time.

Inscape Publishing offers an excellent time-management assessment and tool to focus on developing time-management skills. It is referenced in the assessment guide in Appendix B. It allows you to assess the following time-management attributes:

Attitudes	Planning	Paperwork
Goals	Scheduling	Delegation
Priorities	Interruptions	Procrastination
Analyzing	Meetings	Teamwork

MY STORY

I learned the value of time management while working in the New York office of the sales president for IBM. His assistant, who knew how to manage his time, controlled his schedule. Sensitive to his priorities, she knew which memos and papers he should see and which should be forwarded to someone else. She decided which meetings were important for him to attend and helped delegate the responsibility to others when necessary. Watching her helped me plan and schedule my time. Subsequently, I made sure that my assistants understood their responsibilities, and I depended on them to help me accomplish my objectives by appropriately managing my calendar.

As I observed the day-to-day activities of the president's assistant, I developed a new level of respect and appreciation for that position. What I previously had considered a mundane job was, next to that of the president, actually the most powerful position in the office. She was the traffic cop who drove the bottom line. She decided who passed go, who went to jail and who was placed in the parking lot. She was a time master. She was the "gatekeeper."

The ability to juggle multiple balls without dropping any can be accomplished by controlling and managing your time. Building solid relationships, mentoring, and developing other skills can be achieved when you *consciously* and *intentionally* value the use of your time.

Managing the calendar also means you have to prioritize and delegate. If you are not going to be in town or if you're with a client, you won't be able to do the work that just came in from the CEO's office. An effective and efficient assistant will make sure you know about the assignment and then help you delegate it. Think of delegation not as passing off work, but rather as an opportunity to provide a learning experience and give exposure to another colleague. View work as opportunities to develop yourself and others.

It is important to be organized so that you can complete the work you've outlined as central to your responsibilities and commitments. It is imperative that your work be completed in a professional and timely manner and be delivered before or on deadline. Lack of time should never be an excuse for a less-than-exceptional deliverable.

What do you do if you have no one to whom you can delegate work? Revisit your priorities. Ask yourself, "What is the end I have in mind?" Adjust accordingly.

COACHABLE MOMENTS

There are times when we need to make time to *be still* so that we can regroup and re-energize. Now that technology makes us accessible around the clock, we really need to schedule "downtime." We need to know how and when to turn off the pager, turn off the cell phone, and make time *not* to be available. To make that happen, you need a back-up plan; you need to have a person who covers you in your absence or a team member with whom you can share responsibility. A support network allows you to understand *consciously* and *intentionally* the value of managing your time.

THE FINAL THOUGHT . . . TIME MANAGEMENT

We need to learn patience. All good things come in time. We need to yield to the understanding that our steps are ordered, and we must sometimes wait for the purpose to be revealed. Schedule some wait time on your calendar. Consider it downtime, which, if scheduled *consciously* and *intentionally*, can be some of the most productive time in your life.

You have the power to command your Time Management. Use it.

TIME MANAGEMENT

LESSONS LEARNED (NUGGETS)

1 _____
2 _____
3 _____

CHECKLIST

- ☐ 1   Timely in attendance or ahead of schedule
- ☐ 2   Establishes a comfortable pace that achieves goals
- ☐ 3   Meets project deadlines
- ☐ 4   Completes tasks in a quality manner
- ☐ 5   Prioritizes personal schedule
- ☐ 6   Develops and communicates action plan to achieve goals
- ☐ 7   Utilizes resources appropriately to complete tasks
- ☐ 8   Works constructively under time pressure
- ☐ 9   Completed a time management assessment
- ☐ 10   Spends time on legacy priorities
- ☐ 11   Consciously builds self-care into daily routine
- ☐ 12   Maintains a sense of purpose and direction

___ *Total*

ACTIONS PLANNED   COMPLETION DATE

1 _____   _____
2 _____   _____
3 _____   _____
4 _____   _____
5 _____   _____

BARRIERS/BLIND SPOTS

1 _____
2 _____
3 _____

ACHIEVEMENTS

1 _____
2 _____
3 _____

Service is the act of giving of yourself, your time, and your expertise to create value in your community and in the lives of others. It is a means of creating your legacy by giving back from your heart.

SERVICE

One of the hardest things that we can do is one of the most rewarding. That thing is giving. Our legacy isn't determined by our title, our position, or the amount of money we have. Our legacy is determined by how much we give . . . how much we give back . . . how many people we give a "hand up" to. That's legacy.

STEPHANIE PARSON
Vice President, The Walt Disney Company

Anyone blessed with a job has an obligation to give back. "Service," says Children's Defense Fund founder Marian Wright Edelman, "is the price we pay for living on this earth." Service creates a legacy for your life.

Through my involvement with the National Council of Negro Women, I learned very early on how high the bar had been set in living a life of service. It became my beacon for my constant desire to share the talents and skills that I have been blessed to experience.

MY LEGACY MODEL

The unheralded life of Mary McLeod Bethune is the personification of service. Born fifteenth of seventeen children, to parents who had been slaves, she worked tirelessly to ensure for African-Americans the right to an education and freedom from discrimination. One of her personal mottos was to "invest in the human soul; who knows, it may be a diamond in the rough." And she lived by that motto. From establishing a school for girls, financed by selling sweet potato pies, to working for women's and voting rights, Bethune's entire life was based on manifesting a dream that she believed could be. At life's end, she had made her mark by working for three presidents—Calvin Coolidge, Herbert Hoover, and Franklin D. Roosevelt. She had founded a college now known as Bethune-Cookman College in Florida, and she'd established the National Council of Negro Women. Based on the principles and policies that gave her life's work meaning, she wrote a legacy to her people and to her nation that has been one of my bedrock sources of inspiration.

YOUR LEGACY

Who are your sources of inspiration? What energizes your life? What is the legacy you will leave to the world?

_____

_____

_____

_____

_____

_____

_____

_____

_____

_____

_____

_____

_____

_____

_____

_____

_____

_____

_____

_____

_____

_____

_____

_____

_____

_____

_____

MODELING THE WAY

Former U.S. Representatives William Gray and Kweisi Mfume are other models of service—successful people who yielded to their inner call to serve. Both men gave up positions of power, leadership, and responsibility in the U.S. Congress to share their knowledge and expertise with organizations they believed had important missions. Gray, who had an outstanding history of personal and professional accomplishments, is leading the United Negro College Fund (UNCF). As a result of his efforts, UNCF has increased its corporate and individual support, and the fund is expanding opportunities for students to receive higher education at historically black colleges and universities (HBCUs).

Under Mfume's stewardship, the National Association for the Advancement of Colored People (NAACP) has continued to open new pathways. He, too, after living a life of public service, is living now to leave an even stronger legacy. These men have provided energetic and passionate leadership based upon the skills and assets established in earlier careers. Their models of selfless sharing are the cornerstones from which we can build whatever is necessary to improve the human condition.

There also are service-sector jobs. Although they are not defined that way per se, these are jobs in which people are driven by their passion for service, rather than by financial gain. If you were to place monetary value on the work of teachers and some public officials, for example, compensation could never be adequate.

Dr. Janice Gantt Kissner, seventeenth international president of Zeta Phi Beta Sorority, represents another role model. She has spent her life in service to others, whether at the March of Dimes or with the Charles Hayes Family Investment Center or the Urban League. She left Zeta with a legacy of a "community-conscious, action-oriented organization." While that motto consists of few words, I often reflect on the labor of love physically required to create the legacy she left for Zeta. Sometimes, service is intermingled with job responsibility; the exercise of both becomes a matter of the head and the heart.

Ted Childs, vice president of Worldwide Diversity for IBM, is another example of the great service that results from giving one's heart to one's work. In every undertaking, Ted has managed to provide exceptional thought leadership within IBM and to outside groups and constituencies. He has truly "given his heart" to making the world recognize diversity as a true business imperative.

These leaders are a few of my personal role models. They have stretched to create new possibilities beyond those that already exist. Service is a blessing often disguised as a roadblock or as a challenge. Hopefully, we will never forget "from whence we have come."

MY FIRST STEPS IN SERVICE

My foray into the world of service began while I was an undergraduate at Livingstone College. I joined Zeta Phi Beta Sorority. Zeta was founded in 1920 on the campus of Howard University in Washington, D.C., as the sister organization of Phi Beta Sigma Fraternity, Inc. and was the first sorority to have a paid staff and to be constitutionally bound to a fraternity. The sorority also was the first sorority to charter international chapters (West Africa and Germany). Zeta was established to foster the ideals of service, charity, scholarship, civic and cultural endeavors, sisterhood, and "finer womanhood." I was attracted to Zeta because of the sorority's activities, which included providing volunteers to staff community-outreach programs, funding scholarships, supporting organized charities, and promoting legislation for social and civic change.

Within a year of joining, I was elected to the national executive board as its undergraduate member-at-large. That position afforded me the opportunity to travel to cities throughout the United States and to provide leadership and organize and plan activities for collegiate sorority sisters. Zeta exposed me to a large cadre of professional black women and gave me my first taste of independence. Sixteen years later, I would be elected international president of the 100,000-member sorority.

SERVICE AS A CULTIVATED ASSET

Service is the sharing of your financial resources, your time, skills and expertise. It is giving sweat, blood, and tears. It is placing yourself in an environment where you are doing work because you believe, as the biblical parable of the Talents teaches, that to whom much has been given, much is expected.

But as you give, you also receive. You are able to hone and further develop your skills, extend your network, and possibly create greater opportunities for your future. *Conscious* and *intentional* leaders recognize service as an asset that requires cultivation and development. They recognize how much can be done by people with skills and talent who unselfishly lend themselves to a cause or organization because they appreciate the success and opportunities that they have. Their personal mantra is drawn from the words of the spiritual: "If I can help somebody, then my living has not been in vain." They seek to find ways to serve as a leader in environments other than their day-to-day work, an environment in which the rules, policies, and cultures are different. Such service helps them become broad-minded and well-rounded individuals grounded in concerns beyond the profit line.

Some *conscious* and *intentional* leaders also consider working in the service arena as a second career. Many executives who have taken early retirement or buy-out packages have gone back to school to get teaching credentials. Some have taken jobs as heads of social-service organizations. Their business acumen, knowledge of strategic planning, and financial management has helped many organizations grow.

THE COACH APPROACH

Developing service as an asset is a matter of making it a priority. When you make something a priority, you allocate the time. Can you make trade-offs in your current agenda to make time for engagement in a meaningful activity that could make a difference in someone else's life?

Service is lending your name, providing leadership, or demonstrating through example. It can mean taking the opportunity to represent your company at community events or organizational meetings or making the time to share the expertise with which you've been blessed by coaching someone within your company or in a nonprofit organization. Leaders have resources that, when tapped and utilized for service, can create a very powerful force that strengthens whatever organization for which they choose to work. Whether it's your company's charitable contribution campaign or walking as a team to raise money for cancer or AIDS research, your involvement in service endeavors will make a difference.

By lending your name or donating your talents and expertise to help guide the boards of nonprofits, leaders also can bring additional credibility. Your involvement with college students or alumni associations is a message of encouragement and hope; you become a role model for those whose lives you touch.

Many companies offer matching gifts for charitable contributions or set up internal foundations from which organizations can receive resources or grants. Providing community groups or other organizations with access to the administrator of these programs is a valuable contribution. But be sensitive to the possibility of conflicts of interest. When in doubt, seek out your company's legal counsel.

MY STORY

By the time I was elected international president of Zeta Phi Beta, I had acquired a deeper understanding of what service actually delivers. When you dedicate your life to service for others, the people with whom you serve become your extended family; the work you do becomes your passion. The utilization of my professional skills in service to a group of women around the world meant that the sorority's efforts would, in turn, touch the lives of hundreds of thousands of other people around the globe. Service means being the rock tossed in the water whose ripples reverberate endlessly throughout the pond.

During my tenure as international president, it was my personal mission to help Zeta become a "world-class service organization." Our international agenda included awarding scholarships; sending kids to the U.S. Space Camp; supporting an asthma prevention and treatment program in conjunction with the American Lung Association; educating young women and providing prenatal health care and infant needs with the March of Dimes; and championing AIDS awareness and prevention. My experiences not only taught me about the importance of giving of my time and sharing my financial resources, they also helped me understand how giving *gives back* to me. Through my work in Zeta, I was able to build an extensive public-sector and private-sector network of women around the world. When I started Crystal Stairs, my initial client base was a result of some of those relationships.

I also received tremendous gratification from speaking to groups and serving on panels at national conferences. At the National Black MBA Conference, for example, I had the opportunity to share my experiences on a panel called "Lessons in Leadership for African-American Women." The energy of the overflow crowd, seeking knowledge and information, was empowering for me. During those times, whenever I shared "my story" to inspire and motivate audiences to achieve personal greatness, I felt very energized and passionate about my work.

COACHABLE MOMENT

We all have the potential to create life-changing experiences for people through our service, experiences that open possibilities beyond a person's imagination. One of my former colleagues lives her life dedicated to service. Wanda McKenzie not only helps organizations, she also helps others through networking, sharing information and resources. Recently, she received an email from a relative who is in charge of a group of U.S. troops based in Kuwait. The email requested her assistance in asking individuals and organizations to support these young men and women by sending care packages that included phone calling cards, reading materials, specialty foods, and letters. Wanda used her extensive network to forward the email so that people might respond to this urgent need. Because her network often has benefited from her life of service, when Wanda calls, we listen and respond.

THE FINAL THOUGHT . . . SERVICE

Living a life of service means taking responsibility for future generations by nurturing and encouraging them. Service is the foundation of love, the creator of hope and a light of confidence for others. Using faith as its guide, service honors the dignity of others and seeks to create harmony through its works.

Leave a legacy. Eternalize a life of Service!

SERVICE

LESSONS LEARNED (NUGGETS)

1 _____
2 _____
3 _____

CHECKLIST

☐   1   Knows what "wakes you up inside"
☐   2   Actively engaged in charitable causes
☐   3   Provides financial support to areas of passion
☐   4   Serves as a role model
☐   5   Uses skills from professional training in community work
☐   6   Provides leadership in achieving vision and mission of teams
☐   7   Energy is focused on activities that establish a legacy
☐   8   Leverages resources to benefit charitable endeavors
☐   9   Extends professional network to service
☐ 10   Nurtures future generations
☐ 11   Creates life-changing experiences for people
☐ 12   Identifies talent and strengthens it through service
___ *Total*

ACTIONS PLANNED   COMPLETION DATE

1 _____   _____
2 _____   _____
3 _____   _____
4 _____   _____
5 _____   _____

BARRIERS/BLIND SPOTS

1 _____
2 _____
3 _____

ACHIEVEMENTS

1 _____
2 _____
3 _____

The energy that we exert on our work plan and our life plan is an equation that sometimes changes based on shifts in priorities. At any given moment, you have to choose the weight of the numerator and denominator that make up that equation by determining what's *most* important. It means setting priorities while being flexible in order to work your plan.

WORK/LIFE EQUATION

When we build self-care into our daily habits, self-care becomes ingrained in our being. The longer we work, we take energy away from our bodies and minds. When we take time out for self-care, we replenish ourselves and create even more energy to do things effortlessly.

AN OBSERVATION BY DONNA COULSON
Coach and Corporate Trainer

Each and every day, by the grace of God, we wake up to fulfill the many roles of our lives. As we try to be so many things to so many people, we must not forget that we need to stop and take care of "self" for when "your cup runneth over," you must take time out to re-charge your battery.

STACIE N. C. GRANT
Founder and CEO, C&G Enterprises

I have a difficult time with the notion of Work/Life balance. That's the *C* in me and my experience talking. So I tapped into my mathematical memory bank and decided to call this asset "Work/Life Equation." As you think about the denominator and the numerator, how you apply the numbers and the weighting is your choice.

You need to make *conscious* and *intentional* choices about how you divide your time. It means making decisions as to what's *most* important. It means setting priorities. Just as writing your annual performance plan at work is important to your professional development, creating goals and objectives for what you want to accomplish in your personal life also is critical.

As in business, when you are clear about your purpose, mission, objectives, and performance targets, you can make the best possible *conscious* and *intentional* decision about how to achieve the objectives you have set. Once you make a plan, it becomes the framework for making choices. By keeping track of your progress on a monthly basis, it also becomes the tool you use to measure how you're managing your life.

The Life Compass© is an assessment for pointing north in your life. Curvie Burton, an Electronic Data Systems (EDS) executive and ITSMF leader, introduced me to his circles of life, from which I adapted this assessment. In ITSMF, his passion for having members check-in and check-out was used to bridge the personal and professional circles that changed during the interim period of the organization's quarterly meetings. The result was phenomenal sharing of experiences that yielded personal and professional transformations.

THE CRYSTAL STAIRS LIFE COMPASS©

Look at the graphic on the next page and complete it according to the instructions. Let's work a bit with your compass by considering a couple of scenarios. You decide that you will spend more time with your family. Now, suppose you are offered a promotion to launch a new project for your company. The promotion requires that you move out of town. You will receive a pay increase, but you will have to spend extra time at work with your new team in order to build the infrastructure for the new project, which will take a projected six months. If you have a compass and a personal plan, the framework exists for you to make a decision based on what is in the best interest of your life.

Let's go back to the compass. What do each of the circles mean to you in terms of how you want to allocate your time? Where do you want to be and based on *whose* definition of success? Of course, there are trade-offs you must make when it comes to your work and the rest

CRYSTAL STAIRS LIFE COMPASS©

A plan to live a meaningful life requires taking a look at where you are today relative to where you want to be in any given aspect of your life.

For each area of your life, assess where you are currently on a scale of 0–10. (0 is the bull's-eye of the circle, no place; 10 is the best it could be, the outer circle perimeter.) Place a dot between 0 and 10 to indicate where you are today. Then connect the dots to find the balance of your compass, your life.

Review each and put a dot where you would like to be in the element and connect those dots. The space in between the dots represents the "gap" that you want to bridge.

Prioritize the three largest gaps and take three immediate actions this week to address each of the three. Include a detailed plan as a component of your "journey assessment."

of your life. What trade-offs are you willing to make? If it were a see-saw, would the balance be 80 percent on work and 20 percent on life? Would it be 50–50 or 90–10?

Ultimately, it is your choice. But the challenge is to understand why you make those choices and to be *conscious* of the potential benefits and drawbacks of every decision you make. Head north in life; tackle the east/west detours. Bounce back up when life goes south. Then head north again! Due north!

MY STORY

For most of my career, I worked temporary duty assignments (TDY). It was a conscious choice, the path I believed would help me advance my career. I enjoyed the opportunity to live in different cities and regions of the country, and I took advantage of the culture and lifestyle each area had to offer. When I lived in New York City, I rode the subways, window-shopped on Fifth Avenue, attended numerous black-tie bene-fit dinners, and enjoyed the theater. I worked with the Dance Theater of Harlem and The Boys and Girls Choir of Harlem and met two phe-nomenally talented men, Arthur Mitchell and Dr. Walter Turnbull.

In California, I spent a lot of time at the beach. My clientele includ-ed film studios and many high profile, evolving businesses. I joined a myriad of community and social-service organizations, including the Beverly Hills West Chapter of the Links, Rotary Club in Santa Monica, and a City of Hope committee.

While traveling to and from California on TDY, I realized that after many years of trying, I was finally pregnant! As fate would have it, my fourth-grade boyfriend had become an infertility specialist and had an office in my territory. After several painful tests, Dr. Michael Jones had given me great news: My tubes were cleared. Within weeks, I was expecting!

I had only a year under my belt as a branch manager, which made it very difficult to accept that a major detour in my career was occurring. During a business partner conference in Dallas, I asked Robin Sternbergh, an IBM senior executive, if she could talk with me during a break. Many tears later, she provided me with the best coaching session on earth. Her approach was simple and straightforward: "Let me know when you want to go home to Cincinnati, and don't worry about it." That was a classic coachable moment! Her words instilled in me a fierce loyalty and respect for the IBM Corporation, unshakable to this day. Thanks, Dr. Michael, and thanks, Robin, *Coach extraordinaire!*

Through the TDY assignments, I experienced both economic diversity and economic disparity. I witnessed lifestyles of the rich and the famous while remaining connected to my passion of service to those who were poor and unknown. I was able to witness divergent views of what it means to be happy. The TDYs helped broaden my perspective. Coming from a small town in North Carolina, I was very grateful for the experiences. But more importantly, these experiences humbled me. They helped me develop an even greater reverence for my life and taught me that it was possible to create a life of service, wherever I found myself.

CHALLENGE FOR WOMEN

The paradigm of men being the sole source of financial support for a family has long been broken. With more women in the work force, either as equal financial partners or as sole supporters or contributors for their families, the necessity for developing a *conscious* and *intentional* life compass is even more of an imperative. Women have to set priorities and weigh their choices in order to manage their lives best. Otherwise, it is always an issue of trade-offs. For example, there was a point when corporations were creating innovative approaches to work that gave employees flexibility, such as two people sharing one job. It was a win-win situation for the employees and company. But corporate competition, the shrinking job market, lay-offs, and cutbacks are again forcing employees—particularly women—to make difficult choices. Job security is not a given. If you have a life compass upon which to base your decisions, the process will call upon your vision for life and will remind you not to yield in the heat of the moment.

THE COACH APPROACH

Take a minute and go back to your life compass. What is the life you want to live? How would you define and quantify the work components?

What about your time? What are you willing to do to create the life that matches the compass?

This is your moment of truth.

Too often, we act as if our circumstances dictate our lives when in fact we have choices or options. We may not always like those choices. But they do exist. Let me give you an example. You're working on a team presentation, and you have a family emergency. The work that you've been assigned is an integral component of the project. You have to make a choice. The choice is not between your family emergency and your work. The choice is how you will cover the work that needs to be done *and* take care of the emergency. Hopefully, you've developed relationships with members of your team that are flexible enough to handle emergencies. Having a solid team and support network is a critical component of the Work/Life Equation. (See Chapter 7 on Teamwork.)

Suppose you are an entrepreneur or the head of a community-based organization. Working long hours, sometimes seven days a week, is part of the job description. What does your life compass look like? What trade-offs can you make? Have you come to the fork in the road when you recognize that you are involved in too many activities? How do you make the choices that will continue to drive your passion and the objectives you have established in your life's plan?

There are a series of assessments you can take that will help you set goals and develop a work/life plan. Please review the Guide to Assessments and Tools in Appendix B and make a *conscious, intentional* effort to spend time understanding yourself, your priorities, and the shifts in your life that will be necessary to achieve your goals.

Another approach to planning life's goals is via a book and seminar entitled "Your Best Year Yet." This methodology provides a process to discuss, document, and track your goals systematically. Jinny Ditzler's approach provides "a proven method to making the next twelve months the most successful ever." The logical *DC* mathematician in me wholeheartedly subscribes to this approach. I like the tangible deliverables it produces.

COACHABLE MOMENT

Alana Robinson captured the distinction of being my first "one hundred percent" *dominance* behaving executive that I profiled. For every indicator of *D* that could be selected, she chose it with a secondary preference for *I, influence.* As she read her results and we talked about situations that validated the assessment, she became very aware and attempted to flex when appropriate. What struck me as most revealing was when she requested that her entire family complete the assessment process. She predicted each one to the letter.

The value that Alana gained was an understanding of the dynamics of the family relationships. Her college-age son, very similar to her husband, was a *steadiness* and *conscientiousness* (*SC*) person. His zeal for life was based on enjoying and appreciating a comfortable pace. Her eldest son, a new entrant to the Wall Street work environment of New York City, was aspiring, talented, *dominance* and *influence* (*DI*) oriented, just like his Mom. What advantage does understanding family behavior provide?

Alana, a hard-charging successful executive, now is more sensitive to calibrating her Work/Life Equation. She plays hard and she works hard. But she now knows when to adjust the levers.

With my daughter, I listen now with the ears of a mom with high *DC* behavior interacting with a child who is very much a composite of her *SC* father and me. She extracts both of our *C* behaviors and maps it with her *I* to keep us all grounded in our communication and behavior. I hear her words and I see her actions from the standpoint of her style preferences and now flex to strengthen our communication. In particular, we have established a common, nonthreatening language for our interactions.

I never want to forget what a blessing my daughter is in my life. My mother once told me before my daughter was born that "you don't know love until you have a child." I now understand the love that extends from the umbilical cord of life to the never-ending responsibility and joy of nurturing and loving another human being.

More than anything, I treasure the flexibility and the satisfaction that I derive from my life's work. The pace of my life has slowed while the energy of exploring new opportunities has soared. The accomplishments, while measured in financial reward from the business, also are measured in hugs from my child.

I especially treasure the experience of accompanying my daughter's sixth-grade class of eighty-eight students to White Pines Ranch: A dude ranch just for kids! Waking up to seven inches of snow after our first of two nights provided the environment and atmosphere that was a true adventure. Lifelong memories include riding horses through the snow, cross country skiing, trailblazing through the freshly fallen snow to experience the beauty of the canyon, making my first-ever snow angel, and using a compass for "orienteering." These simple moments awakened the sense of adventure I needed to continue seeking new possibilities and expecting the greatness of the universe to present itself in my life.

I also attended the U. S. Space Camp Parent Child Program. This orchestrated program tested my limits, but I applauded the success of the week when I completed every task assigned, to my daughter's surprise as well as my own. Tremendous memorable moments were created by climbing and descending on the zero-gravity wall; riding the Multi-Axis Trainer (MASTIF); simulating a walk on the moon with the Microgravity Simulator (1/6 Chair); building and launching model rockets; maneuvering inside the "hamster wheel"; and successfully completing our award-winning mission.

The Crystal Stairs Strategic Life Plan Framework© on the next page can provide a method to plan, monitor, and measure your success against the targets you've established for your Work/Life Equation. I challenge you to invest the time in yourself necessary to make your equation reflect the dynamics of your priorities.

THE FINAL THOUGHT . . . WORK/LIFE EQUATION

Many of us have been chasing the myth of work/life balance and getting dizzy in the process. The key is to use the Life Compass© to find *your* north, and calibrate your Work/Life Equation.

STRATEGIC LIFE PLAN FRAMEWORK© (LPF)

VISION								
MISSION								
GOALS		PERSONAL				PROFESSIONAL		
		1.	2.		3.		4.	
STRATEGIES	TASKS		TASKS	Due date	TASKS	Due date	TASKS	Due date
1.		Due date						
2.								
3.								
MEASURES								
GUIDING PRINCIPLES	☐ ☐ ☐ ☐ ☐							

© *Crystal Stairs, Inc.* 2002

WORK/LIFE EQUATION

LESSONS LEARNED (NUGGETS)

1 _____
2 _____
3 _____

CHECKLIST

☐ 1 Uses the "Life Compass" to achieve priorities
☐ 2 Understands work expectations
☐ 3 Effectively rotates due north
☐ 4 Conscious focus on work/life equation
☐ 5 Challenges self to discover new possibilities
☐ 6 Assesses the impact of behavior on others
☐ 7 Builds relationships that support a strong network
☐ 8 Achieves self-care targets
☐ 9 Completes assessments that navigate self understanding
☐ 10 Controls and manages through unanticipated interruptions
☐ 11 Checks in regularly with a personal and professional circle of life
☐ 12 Invites the understanding of others' style in balancing work/life

___ *Total*

ACTIONS PLANNED   COMPLETION DATE

1 _____   _____
2 _____   _____
3 _____   _____
4 _____   _____
5 _____   _____

BARRIERS/BLIND SPOTS

1 _____
2 _____
3 _____

ACHIEVEMENTS

1 _____
2 _____
3 _____

Uncertainty about who you are and what you believe will result in a life buffeted by winds like a kite on a string. Established personal and professional principles become your life's framework and prevent you from unconsciously compromising your values. Maintaining a profile of the major guidelines that frame your life is as important as maintaining a professional file.

PERSONAL AND PROFESSIONAL FRAMEWORK

A father took his boy into a toyshop. The boy squirmed away from his dad and roamed the store. In the back, he discovered a statue of a man made of balloons. The boy looked at it for a minute, and then he drew back his fist and hit the balloon man just as hard as he could. The balloon man fell over, and then popped right back up. The confused boy backed off and looked at the balloon man again. One more time, he hit the balloon man as hard as he could. Again, the man fell over, and again he popped right back up.

The father found his son, just as the boy hit that balloon man for a third time. He asked his son, "Why do you think he comes back up when you hit him and knock him down?"

The boy thought for a minute and said, "I don't know. I guess it's because he's standing up on the inside."

AUTHOR UNKNOWN
The Pastor's Story File

What makes a person stand up on the inside? I think the answer includes having a firm foundation, being grounded in one's beliefs and values. What are your guiding principles? Are you living your faith? Do you know and understand your personal brand? These are just a few of the questions you need to answer in order to develop your Personal and Professional Framework (PPF).

PERSONAL AND PROFESSIONAL FRAMEWORK

PERSONAL
- ❏ Guiding principles
- ❏ Values
- ❏ Spirituality
- ❏ Exclusive signature marketing
- ❏ Elevator speech
- ❏ Extreme self-care plan
- ❏ Financial plan & investments
- ❏ Wills and trust agreements
- ❏ Insurance and health information
- ❏ Retirement information
- ❏ Strategic life plan
- ❏ Others

PROFESSIONAL
- ❏ Vita, resume, bio
- ❏ Salary and earnings history
- ❏ Awards and recognition
- ❏ Business transactions
- ❏ Business documents
- ❏ Speaking engagements
- ❏ Professional involvement
- ❏ Others

PERSONAL FRAMEWORK

Guiding Principles

What are your landmarks in life that point you due north? Do they include truth? Honesty? Fairness? Integrity? Being clear about your guiding principles will help you become consistent in the rest of your life and will prevent you from unconsciously or unintentionally compromising your value system. Guiding principles are the rules you live by no matter what the situation.

Spirituality

For many people, spirituality is part of their PPF. During my corporate life, I never took the opportunity to understand or fully develop my spirituality. In corporate circles, talking about spiritual beliefs was often considered out of bounds.

During the strategic development phase of Crystal Stairs, Wanda McKenzie, an IBM marketing executive, shared with me the book *The Prayer of Jabez* by Bruce Wilkinson which had been given to her by

Jacquelyn Gates, vice president of human resources at Duke Energy. Taken from 1 Chronicles 4:10, the biblical passage reads:

And Jabez called on the God of Israel, saying, Oh that thou wouldest bless me indeed, and enlarge my coast, and that thine hand might be with me, and that thou wouldest keep me from evil, that it may not grieve me! And God granted him that which he requested.

After reading that verse, I began to pray about it, and it was through prayer that I came to realize that I could control my destiny. I needed vision, wisdom, courage, and determination to act. In many ways, that was a moment of *spiritual awakening*. I began to sense that there was a greater plan for my life, that God had other work for me to do. I was just opening my eyes to see the light shining on my new path, eyes that had never before consciously witnessed the Spirit at work during my career at IBM.

Living your faith should be a part of your foundation. Using prayer or meditation for guidance is a way of reconnecting with who you are and what is important to you. It is important that you be so grounded that your heart and soul emerge as part of your behavior, leadership, and management style. When you don't have to split your personalities between your personal and professional lives, you have a peace of mind that permeates every facet of your life. You must consistently maintain the same high level of truth, honesty, fairness, and integrity when conducting business with partners, clients, and/or customers. Whether it's a verbal commitment sealed with a handshake or an exchange of email, your word can't be negotiable. Otherwise, your foundation is as stable as a crystal vase of flowers sitting on an open window ledge.

MY STORY

I had two experiences involving small businesses whose owners did not live up to their word. They left me holding the ball with considerable expenses that I incurred on behalf of their businesses that they did not reimburse; expenses I incurred based on good faith agreements. At the time, I did not recognize that these business owners and I did not share the same values. In hindsight, I admit that I did not pay attention to my intuition, which was red-flagging these relationships. Fortunately, I was able to extricate myself before my reputation suffered. I did not want to be identified with firms that lacked the core values of truth, integrity, fairness, and honesty. Both instances provided valuable lessons in the importance of listening to my heart and soul, honoring my foundation, and never, ever straying from my personal values in the course of doing business.

Your Personal and Professional Framework also contributes to your ability to win business, build strong customer relationships, and even strengthen partnerships that are critical to your personal growth or business success. Never forget: What goes around comes around!

I thank God that I am grounded in my faith, in my own guiding principles—living and walking in truth, treating people fairly, manifesting integrity, and living honestly. That combination of guiding principles and spirituality has bridged many gaps in my life and has afforded me a deeper appreciation for the need always to be true to myself. Having survived many negative situations, I am driven to do a little truth-saying on this topic: To corporate and community gossipers, male and female, the energy that you expend in negative and false communications not only damages others, it also hurts you. Instead, invest positive energy that can be used to build up and strengthen others as well as yourself.

I encourage my clients not to allow the negative energy of others to slow them in their journey, nor to be barriers in the road. I advocate positive energy as a source of renewed strength for personal transformation and professional development.

Exclusive Signature Marketing

I also urge you to think of your personal foundation as your exclusive signature. Most brand managers make *conscious* and *intentional* efforts to mold and shape their products. In this case, what *conscious* and *intentional* efforts can you make to mold and shape your personal signature? How would someone who has known you for a very long time describe you, versus someone who has met you for the first time? How do you introduce yourself? Is it by title? Position? Company? Neighborhood? Do you talk about the achievements of your spouse and children, rather than your own?

For some people, their personal signature incorporates their attire. It can reflect great taste or extreme taste. Be very conscious of the distinction because whatever it is, people will tend to identify it with you. For example, I usually wear a pin. Many people remember or recognize me because of my pins. I recently discovered that some things about our personal signature travel even through generations. My grandmother, for example, also loved pins. After her death, when all of my relatives had taken everything they thought of great monetary value, what remained was something I dearly treasure—a costume-jewelry pin. I never connected the generational links in personal signatures until I discovered a handwritten letter from my grandmother and recognized the similarities between her signature and mine when we wrote the cursive E. That was the beginning of my "Exclusive Signature Marketing" branding journey.

Making sure that your exclusive signature is consistent can be costly. You have to know how to get the best value for your dollar. I tend to wear conservative attire, by the same designer. I am usually dressed on the conservative side of what is appropriate for the occasion and prefer not to be trapped by the "business casual" label. In order to create my exclusive signature, I had to develop a sound financial plan. Every purchase became an investment in my personal foundation and exclusive signature.

Work with a personal shopper who knows and understands your tastes as well as your style. While shopping for a Christmas gift for a client, the client's Personal Image and Wardrobe Coach at Robert Vance Ltd. in Chicago was very helpful in selecting gifts that represented the classic distinction of my client's exclusive signature. It was an automatic home run, making Jay Rosenthal a coach of great value to my client and to me. For someone trying to develop an exclusive signature, a coach or personal shopper like Jay should be a consideration. The key is to find one who best matches and understands the image that is part of your personal signature.

It is imperative that your exclusive signature be consistent across the board—in your written communications, in the marketing materials you distribute about yourself (your résumé, your biography, or your executive photograph, etc.). The way you present yourself should create a consistent portrait of your exclusive signature, no matter where you are.

Tom Peters' book *Brand You 50: Reinventing Work* provides tremendous insight into the power of personal branding.

THE COACH APPROACH

Another part of your personal foundation is your team of supporters. In some coaching circles, this is referred to as your Team 100™. Your team is a vast network of professional and personal resources in five categories: Business and Work, Money and Legal, Personal Health, Personal Services, and Extreme Self-Care. The goal is, within a year, to comprise a list with names and contact numbers in all of these categories. Team members range from business consultants and financial planners to doctors and massage therapists. As you build a personal framework, think of your team. Who would be on that list? To whom do you turn, for example, for business consultation, financial planning, spiritual guidance, real estate, legal advice, or a personal makeover? How do you nurture and develop that component of your personal foundation? Appendix B provides information about accessing the Team 100™ assessment.

Elevator Speech

If you have as much difficulty as I do in answering the "So what do you do?" question, take time to develop a thirty-second elevator speech. This is a statement that you make to introduce yourself to engage in conversation. Be sure that it focuses on you as a person and not on your titles or other fleeting descriptions. What is a defining statement that represents you and opens the door for continued conversation? Practice until you can crisply state your purpose in life.

PROFESSIONAL FRAMEWORK

Professional Tool Kit

In your professional tool kit, it is important to always maintain a current copy of your vita. That vita should be the history of your professional *and* personal life. From the vita, you can then create targeted résumés and biographies. Résumés and biographies *always* should be customized to the audience.

Your professional tool kit should contain your salary and earnings history, appraisals, client letters, team and/or individual thank-you notes, announcements about your professional advancements, news articles that have been published about you, journal articles you have written, and professional photographs of you in different environments.

Professional File

Maintain a file of your personal and professional business transactions. The file should include all legal documents, agreements, financial records, tax filings, insurance, health records, and property transactions. Include in your professional file an inventory of your property and a copy of receipts of major purchases. Although it is a challenge to organize the system, it will pay huge dividends.

Maintain a list of all speaking engagements conducted as a part of your job or while providing community service. The list should include: title, target audience, size, location, and other key notes. Also start a library of video and audiotapes of your speaking and/or training engagements. This material can become the foundation for your "next career."

Professional Involvement

Know the market, know your business, and know your competition. Be cognizant of your demeanor at all times and be certain that you do not inappropriately blend the lines of personal and professional. There are times when you may be able to mingle business with pleasure safely, such as traveling with a spouse or adding extra days to the front or back end of a business trip. Other opportunities might include participation in professional associations, conventions, or events such as *Black Enterprise* Magazine's Golf and Tennis Challenge.

I also endorse events such as Odyssey Network. It provides opportunities for learning while networking and relaxing in a supportive environment. A myriad of conferences are available for professional development, such as the National Black MBA Association's annual conference, the National Association of Black Accountants (NABA), the National Association of Women Business Owners (NAWBO), the International Coach Federation (ICF) Annual Conference, and others that relate to special interest groups with which you may be associated. Within the fraternity and sorority community, there are many opportunities to learn and network: Boulé (national meetings), conclaves, and regional, state, and local conferences all have agendas that encourage professional and personal development.

Create business and personal opportunities through small network events within your community or by bringing together members of your network. Remember the Friday night "family potluck dinners" at

church? Initiate potluck dinners in your home, or invite a group
to a restaurant for dinner. Explore groups such as Rotary Club or
"Leadership (name of your city)" as a means of broadening your network.

A central part of your professional foundation is to have impeccable
skills, which is discussed in depth in the chapter on Performance. But
maintain an inventory of skills you have developed, classes you have
taken, and projects on which you have worked that have increased your
knowledge or enhanced your development. This is an excellent source
to develop your ongoing lifelong learning plan.

THE COACH APPROACH TO
THE PERSONAL TOUCH

Essential to both your personal and professional foundation is the ability and the foresight to be able to recognize, acknowledge, and thank
people. Keep a file of all-occasion cards both at home and in your
office. Both files should include birthday, anniversary, wedding, baby
shower, birth, get well, sympathy, thank-you, and congratulations
cards. Keep a stock of blank cards, too, so that you can write your own
messages.

While attending an Odyssey Network retreat in Palm Desert with
more than 350 affluent minority women who had gathered for personal self-care and professional development, I was sitting in the front row
of a workshop. Just before it began, public relations and marketing
maven Terrie Williams walked in and sat next to me. During the session, I asked several questions, and Terrie and I swapped a few comments. A few months later, we met again at *Black Enterprise* Magazine's
Entrepreneur's Conference. Six months after that, we met again at
ITSMF's conference in Jamaica. Each time, we continued our conversation as if it had ended the week before. What's so amazing to me is that
no matter how busy Terrie is (and this woman *is* busy), she continues
to embody and truly live by the principles she espouses in her book *The
Personal Touch*. I think her advice on "Tips for Success That Guarantee
You Will Stand Out Over Everyone Else" is invaluable:

➤ Know that your reputation is valuable.
➤ Do what you say you are going to do.

➤ Return telephone calls.

➤ Know your profession—be visible.

➤ Develop a knack for remembering names.

➤ Create a "small talk" notebook.

➤ Send a follow-up note.

➤ Go through your Rolodex periodically—just to stay in touch.

➤ Selectively donate your services.

➤ Remember to say "Thank you."

➤ Read at least one newspaper a day.

EXTREME SELF-CARE

I had the opportunity to attend Odyssey Network 2002 and dedicate some time for my own spiritual and intellectual renewal. With two years of entrepreneurship under my wings, my energy was being fueled by excess adrenaline and I truly needed the down time. I took to heart the advice of consultant Audra Bohannon, whose opening session had the theme "Making Choices. . . A Life Without Regrets." She challenged the participants to think about life as a stage for adventure and engagement.

When I forgot about my work long enough to be open to what was going on all around me, I could hear the voices of my fellow Odyssey sisters and deeply listened. I recognized the similarities of our challenges. We all struggle to reach various milestones in our lives. We all constantly recreate our image, rediscover and redefine the terms for happiness, and reevaluate what it means to be true to ourselves.

During our time together at Odyssey Network 2002, Divine Intervention helped us release our challenges and let our spirits soar. Whether it was a new hair style (which I took advantage of thanks to the magnificent hair stylist James Adams, owner of Renovarie Hair Salon in Birmingham, Alabama), riding in hot air balloons, or watching the sunset from atop a horse, we engaged in new adventures that not only transformed but also healed us.

As a result, I have made a solemn pledge that my annual renewal and energy boost will be *conscious* and *intentional* time spent with the Odyssey Network sisters. Thanks to Linda Spradley Dunn, founder and CEO of Idamar Enterprises, for creating the Odyssey Network opportunity in surroundings that invite extreme self-care.

I appreciate and support opportunities to pamper my mind, body, and spirit. Spa retreats are great ways to engage in extreme self-care. Whether for a day or several days, we all need an emotional and mental shift away from our day-to-day challenges. It gives us time to create our own space, where we can define who we are: our passions, our gifts and talents, what wakes us up in the morning, and why we are blessed to walk on this earth.

If you can't take several days to participate in a structured retreat, you certainly can create your *own* routine. Regularly scheduled time on your calendar for yourself—from hair, manicures, pedicures, and massages to taking yourself out to your favorite restaurant or curling up with a book—is *conscious* and *intentional* extreme self-care critical to your personal and professional well-being.

Be sure to schedule time for vacations! During my twenty-two years at IBM, I thought I was indispensable. A vacation was foreign to my work ethic. I remember taking a cell-phone call one morning from a client while at Animal Kingdom on a family vacation. My family went on without me, and I lost them for the rest of the day! Subsequently, I've learned that those who use vacations to rejuvenate have broken the code. We owe it to ourselves and to the people in our lives, from our colleagues to our family, to take time off to renew and refresh. There is no trophy given for how much vacation you didn't take. Winners take all!

THE FINAL THOUGHT . . .
PERSONAL AND PROFESSIONAL FRAMEWORK

Building a solid personal and professional framework begins with an objective review of where you are now. If you aren't standing up on the inside, what do you need to change? Working with a coach can provide you with insight and oversight as you analyze your strengths and challenges and develop a plan for personal and professional growth. This critical asset is the foundation for your life. Make sure you pour deep cement.

Crystallize your Personal and Professional Framework!

PERSONAL AND PROFESSIONAL FRAMEWORK

LESSONS LEARNED (NUGGETS)

1 _____
2 _____
3 _____

CHECKLIST

- ☐ 1 Treats people with honesty, integrity, and respect
- ☐ 2 Maintains a high standard of professional behavior
- ☐ 3 Ensures sensitive information remains confidential
- ☐ 4 Learns and acquires new information
- ☐ 5 Maintains a skills development plan
- ☐ 6 Acts in accordance with company policies and procedures
- ☐ 7 Holds sacred personal core values
- ☐ 8 Remains calm and collected when situations get stressful
- ☐ 9 Organizes and files key personal and professional records
- ☐ 10 Establishes and brands a personal exclusive signature
- ☐ 11 Recognizes and invites divine intervention
- ☐ 12 Engages and nurtures Team 100™

___ *Total*

ACTIONS PLANNED   COMPLETION DATE

1 _____   _____
2 _____   _____
3 _____   _____
4 _____   _____
5 _____   _____

BARRIERS/BLIND SPOTS

1 _____
2 _____
3 _____

ACHIEVEMENTS

1 _____
2 _____
3 _____

THE NEVER-ENDING JOURNEY

WHERE DO YOU GO FROM HERE?

Now that you have the insight and the tools to head *due north*, I encourage you to engage *consciously* and *intentionally* in the Crystal Stairs Leadership Journey. To get started, respond to the following:

➤ Identify three gaps or blind spots that you discovered as you studied the Leadership Assets™. Do you need a "truth-saying" session? Who will be your confidante?

➤ Determine the three assessments that would be most helpful for you to take and review with a coach in the next thirty days. What outrageous requests would cause a shift due to your awareness?

➤ Identify five situations in the next week that relate to your specific behavior style and five situations in which you observe a specific behavior style in others. What does flexing look like and feel like?

➤ Increase your Conscious and Intentional Barometer™ measure. What needs to change in your life?

➤ Check your Personal and Professional Framework against your Life Compass. How solid is your foundation for "orienteering" your life and steering it due north?

➤ Recognize three "coachable moments" in your life right now.

Are you coachable? Have you engaged a coach? What barrier is in your way? What's your next step?

➢ Champion lifelong learning. Have you documented the specific areas in which you want to extend your reach and understanding? How will you accomplish these goals?

➢ Prepare your Assessment Profile. What "Insights to Success®" have you gained? What is a major next step?

➢ Wrestle with all of the elements of self-awareness that are aligned with your vision of life. Has your Work/Life Equation been calibrated?

➢ Review your Journey Assessment. What is the first of the Leadership Assets™ that you will trigger, with "maniacal focus," to strengthen?

➢ List three stories that you would share related to the Leadership Assets™. Have you shared your stories with others through Crystal Stairs?

➢ Commit to join the Crystal Stairs Leadership Journey. What step(s) will you take *now* to execute your plan?

THE CRYSTAL STAIRS LEADERSHIP JOURNEY

This book is my compass for *Due North!* It has helped me share my passion and lessons learned while enabling me to "bucketize" my life experiences and develop the 12 Leadership Assets™. I am confident that by spending time to develop your assets, you will receive a return on your investment in yourself. I am committed to traveling with you on your journey. Please send up a flare anytime you can't find due north!

ACKNOWLEDGMENTS

MY METAPHOR FOR LIFE

At Livingstone College, Dr. Lakin also introduced me to the book *The Learning Tree*, a novel by Gordon Parks Sr. I developed a metaphor for viewing life as a constant opportunity to grow and learn. Lifelong learning became the key ingredient in my life plan. In *Due North!* my journey is recorded as a way to help others grow and learn. In addition to my experiences, I've shared the words and wisdom of experts who have helped guide my journey. I learned many years ago that "No (wo)man is an island," and it is important that we always acknowledge and thank those who have been torchbearers on our path. To that end, I would like to offer accolades and share some closing thoughts.

As I look back on this story about my journey, I realize I have been the beneficiary of many amazing blessings. There have been Divine Interventions that have transformed my life, including those that came when I did not necessarily want them. I have certainly lived the promise of the song performed so eloquently by Donnie McClurkin, "We Fall Down, But We Get Up," and I am, like the title of the song so passionately sung by Teddy Pendergrass, "Truly Blessed." I would ask that you think about the blessings in your life as I share a few of mine.

SCHOOL DAYS

I believe that much of who I am was molded and grounded in my family's value system and what I learned in school—Monroe Street

Elementary School, Knox Jr. High School, Price High School, Salisbury High School, Livingstone College, Indiana University at Bloomington, and Corporate Coach University International.

To my teachers, I only hope and pray that one day we will live in a society where appropriate compensation is given to those who are the true engineers of life, teachers. *I thank all the teachers who have ever shared their knowledge so that I might learn.*

Many administrators created environments that were conducive to learning and eased the tasks necessary to matriculate at academic institutions. Your hard work and personal commitment made a difference. The glue that you provided bonded students and established friendships for life. To my classmates and dear friends, *thanks* for your spirit and love.

FAMILY

To my "blood" parents and to my adult adopted parents, *thank you, with love.* To Anjylla, Stan, Dollie, Maxine, Julius, John, James, Carter, Will, Colethia, Susie, Wanda, Barbara, Kim, Vercilla, Doris, Monica, Dasiy, Marilyn, Karen, Woody, and every member of my very large "blood" family and extended family, *I love you.*

I also must acknowledge my church families, beginning with Trinity United Presbyterian, previously known as Church Street Presbyterian; New Prospect Baptist in Cincinnati; and now DuPage AME, located in Chicago. You are the pillars of my foundation from which I continue to draw strength. *Thanks!*

"It's my family" is a special network of incredibly talented and grounded individuals. You have given me wings of energy. *Thanks, ITSMF!*

One is blessed who has neighbors who are with you every step of the way. To those who currently live, or have lived in close proximity, I appreciate you.

BUSINESS ASSOCIATES

Colleagues at IBM nurtured, sheltered, and prepared me for passage along the magnificent road that I am now traveling. I often think about writing a very long letter and personally acknowledging all of the tremendous men and women who provided light on my path at IBM across the world. The letter would be emailed to team members, mentors, managers, leaders, and coaches. This technique would be counter to our learning of stretching to keep technology personal. So, let's try this approach. If our paths have ever crossed, pick up a rock. Hold it in your hand. Think of it as a "touchstone." When you touch it, feel my hug, my heart, my mind, and my soul saying *"Thank you."*

At IBM, there were many clients and business partners who trusted my involvement with their businesses. We established relationships and friendships for which I will be eternally grateful. As an entrepreneur, the engagements continue as we work together to achieve your goals, dreams, and objectives. I appreciate your confidence and your commitment to the mission of "strengthening your Leadership Assets™."

Thanks to Inscape Publishing, Target Training International, and Wonderlic for your superb services as partners.

ZETA PHI BETA SORORITY INC. AND THE NATIONAL PAN-HELLENIC COUNCIL

This list would have to reprint the thousands of names in the Zeta Directory to appropriately trace the path of my journey. It is also the one list that if I were to start naming names and missed one, I would never hear the end of it. So, suffice it to say, to everyone in the "blue and white family," sisterly and brotherly love to you forever.

I appreciate our founders, our past presidents, and the Zeta chapters that I have been privileged to be a member of in Salisbury, Cincinnati, Los Angeles, and Chicago.

To the "World Class Service Leadership Team" who served during the 1992–1996 administration in local, state, regional, and national offices, you were the backbone, as well as the committed members who energized our members to serve our communities. Thanks for embracing the vision.

To the regional directors—Doris M. Stokes, chair; Nathalia M. East Roberts, Dr. Nell Williams Ingram, Laura Farwell, Bessie Canty, Rosie Thompson, Norma Collins, Lisa Givens, Dr. Rosalind Hale, Marilyn Brooks—you exemplified Zeta at her best. *I will always love you!*

While I served as the international president of Zeta, I also was cognizant of the notion of being "everyone's Grand." To those in the sisterhood of Zeta, the brothers of Phi Beta Sigma, and to *all* of the other seven organizations of the Pan-Hellenic Council, it was a privilege to serve. You are the source of memories that will last a lifetime.

To the youth groups and undergraduate sisters and brothers, there will always be changes, opportunities for growth, and opportunities to deepen your understanding. The key is to always be prepared. This book will help you on your journey. No matter what the barriers, roadblocks, or obstacles, just remember to keep climbing.

There is one true understanding that I attempted to personify during my leadership journey as Grand Basileus and it surfaces as paramount to lift on the pages of this book . . . *"To God Be the Glory!"*

MY TEAM 100™

There is no substitute for professional care! I have been fortunate to work with individuals who magnify their talents. Of special note: Tina Colbert and LaShawna Richardson, my hair managers, and Renee Hodges, Bessie's Beauty Salon owner, who keep life real; Amy Castanada, my assessment center executive and a person of great spiritual shared values; Donna Coulson, my executive coach who continues to find that stimulating question of the week; Dr. Elbert J. T. Nelson, who delivered the most precious gift in my life; and Clarence Smith, my phenomenal web expert and business advisor.

This book was the product of a great team of individuals. My thanks to Jeri Love, a tremendous visionary and writer who believed in Crystal Stairs and the Leadership Journey; the Jenkins Group team for your publishing expertise; Mary Watson, creator of the pin that inspired the Crystal Stairs logo; and Doretha Curtis, MAC makeup artist who put a face to the name. *Thanks!*

One of my greatest inspirations is the constant reminder of the beauty of the world and the creative energy that can emerge. I often reflect on the art that I have placed on walls throughout my home for many years. I wanted to especially acknowledge the following artists extraordinaire: Leonard and Beverly Freeman, Johana, Thomas Blackshear, Annie Lee, Joe Bray, Gilbert Young, James Donaldson, and Felix O. Eboigbe. Your work gives meaning to visions.

Thank you to every individual who has carried a torch!

LEADERSHIP ASSETS™ JOURNEY ASSESSMENT

This chart provides a summary of the checklists from the end of each chapter. Complete the instructions to prioritize the gaps and determine your focus.

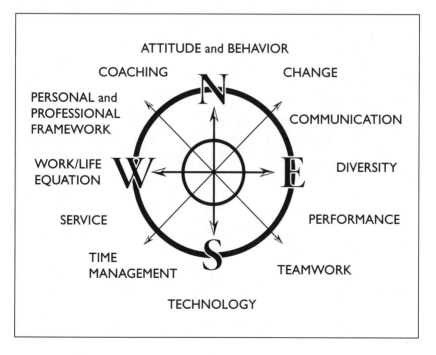

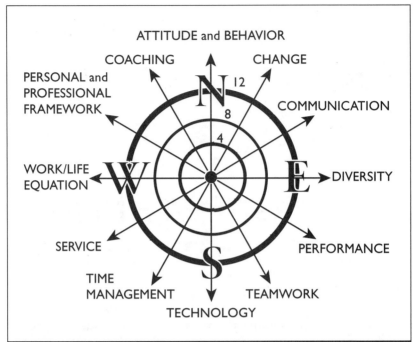

STEP 1: Plot where you are on each arrow pointing to an asset. (The number should be determined by the number of checkmarks total on the Leadership Asset™ Action Plan at the end of each chapter in *Due North!*) Record each number beside each asset on the Journey Chart. Then, plot the point where you would like to be in the next 90 to 180 days relative to the asset. Shade the "gap."

STEP 2: Review your Life Compass© along with your Journey Assessment Summary and determine the top three assets that you want to work on. Select one and place it on your action calendar.

JANUARY	FEBRUARY	MARCH	APRIL
MAY	JUNE	JULY	AUGUST
SEPTEMBER	OCTOBER	NOVEMBER	DECEMBER

INTENTIONAL ACTION	*By when*	MEASURE OF SUCCESS
❏ 1.		
❏ 2.		
❏ 3.		
❏ 4.		
❏ 5.		
REVELATIONS		
❏ 1.		
❏ 2.		
❏ 3.		
❏ 4.		
❏ 5.		
SHIFTS		
❏ 1.		
❏ 2.		
❏ 3.		
❏ 4.		
❏ 5.		

GUIDE TO ASSESSMENTS AND TOOLS

Throughout *Due North!* references have been made to assessments and tools that will provide greater awareness. The following charts provide recommended resources based on the 12 Leadership Assets™.

a = Coaching
b = Attitude and Behavior
c = Change
d = Communication
e = Diversity
f = Performance
g = Teamwork
h = Technology
i = Time Management
j = Service
k = Work/Life Equation
l = Personal and Professional Framework

Contact Crystal Stairs, Inc. for information on any of the assessments or tools listed.

www.Crystal-Stairs.com
Assessment@Crystal-Stairs.com
630-734-1481

ASSESSMENTS AND TOOLS

Crystal Stairs, Inc.

Assessment / Tool	Coaching (a)	Attitude/Behavior (b)	Change (c)	Communication (d)	Diversity (e)	Performance (f)	Teamwork (g)	Technology (h)	Time Management (i)	Service (j)	Work/Life Equation (k)	Pers./Prof. Framework (l)	PERSONAL STATUS (Record results)	NOTES
☐ Leadership Assets™ Development Framework©	a	b	c	d	e	f	g	h	i	j	k	l		
☐ Conscious/Intentional Barometer©	a	b	c	d	e	f	g	h	i	j	k	l		
☐ Tech Checklist©	a							h			k			
☐ Life Compass©	a	b	c	d	e	f	g	h	i	j	k	l		
☐ Leadership Journey Assessment Summary©	a	b	c	d	e	f	g	h	i	j	k	l		
☐ Life Plan Framework©	a	b	c	d	e	f	g	h	i	j	k	l		
☐ Performance Plan©	a	b	c	d	e	f		h	i		k	l		
☐ Development Plan©	a	b	c	d		f		h	i		k	l		
☐ Personal and Professional Framework©	a	b	c	d	e	f	g	h	i	j	k	l		
☐ Coaching Action Plan©	a	b	c	d	e	f	g	h	i	j	k	l		
☐ Crystal Stairs Cultural Assessment	a	b	c	d	e	f	g	h	i	j	k	l		
☐ Wonderlic Multi-Source Feedback Survey for Crystal Stairs Leadership Assets	a	b	c	d	e	f	g	h	i	j	k	l		

ASSESSMENTS AND TOOLS

Assessments and Tools	Coaching	Attitude/Behavior	Change	Communication	Diversity	Performance	Teamwork	Technology	Time Management	Service	Work/Life Equation	Pers./Prof. Framework	PERSONAL STATUS (Record results)	NOTES
Coach U														
□ Team 100™	a	b	c	d	e		g					l		
□ Certified Communicator Program™	a	b	c	d	e							l		
□ Clean Sweep™	a	b	c	d										
Harrell Performance Systems, Inc.														
□ Attitude Assessment©	a	b	c	d								l		
CoachWorks, International														
□ The Coaching Checklist©	a	b	c	d		f								
□ Inside Out Shifts: A Coaching Model©	a	b	c	d		f						l		
VISTA COACH and Trilogy Coaching Institute														
□ The Top 10 High Impact Team Practices©	a	b	c	d		f	g							
Myers Briggs Type Indicator (Personality Assessment)	a	b	c	d							k	l		

ASSESSMENTS AND TOOLS

Inscape Publishing

	Coaching	Attitude/Behavior	Change	Communication	Diversity	Performance	Teamwork	Technology	Time Management	Service	Work/Life Equation	Pers./Prof. Framework	PERSONAL STATUS (Record results)	NOTES
☐ Personal Profile System®—DiSC® Behavior	a	b	c	d	e	f	g	h	i	j	k	l		
☐ I-Sight®—Youth DiSC® Behavior	a	b	c	d	e	f	g	h	i	j	k			
☐ Biblical Profile	a	b	c	d	e	f	g				k			
☐ Role Behavior Analysis	a	b	c	d	e	f	g							
☐ Interpersonal Profile (360° Feedback for Behavior)	a	b	c	d	e	f	g			j	k			
☐ Managing Work Expectations—Transforming Attitudes	a	b	c	d	e	f	g		i	j	k	l		
☐ Transition—The Personal Path Through Change	a	b	c	d	e	f			i	j	k	l		
☐ Focus Point®	a	b	c	d	e		g				k			
☐ Points of View	a	b	c	d	e	f	g				k			
☐ Discovering Diversity Profile®	a	b	c	d		f	g							
☐ Coping and Stress Profile®	a	b	c	d		f	g				k			

ASSESSMENTS AND TOOLS

Inscape Publishing

Tool	Coaching	Attitude/Behavior	Change	Communication	Diversity	Performance	Teamwork	Technology	Time Management	Service	Work/Life Equation	Pers./Prof. Framework	PERSONAL STATUS (Record results)	NOTES
☐ Dimensions of Leadership Profile®	a	b	c	d	e	f	g			j				
☐ Innovate with C.A.R.E. Profile®	a	b	c	d	e	f	g				k			
☐ Time Mastery Profile®	a			d		f	g		i		k			
☐ Personal Listening Profile®	a	b	c	d	e	f	g				k			
☐ Personal Learning Insights Profile®	a	b	c	d	e	f			i					
☐ DiSC® Relationship Profile	a	b	c	d	e	f	g	h						
☐ DiSC® Sales Action Planner	a	b	c	d	e	f	g		i		k	l		
☐ DiSC® Management Action Planner	a	b		d	e	f	g		i		k			
☐ DiSC® Talk! Action Planner	a	b		d	e	f	g		i					
☐ DiSC® Customer Service Action Planner	a	b	c	d	e	f	g		i					
☐ DiSC® Managing Performance Planner	a	b	c	d	e	f	g		i		k			
☐ Adventures in Attitude®	a	b	c	d	e	f	g				k	l		

ASSESSMENTS AND TOOLS

Target Training International (TTI) Ltd.

Assessment	Coaching	Attitude/Behavior	Change	Communication	Diversity	Performance	Teamwork	Technology	Time Management	Service	Work/Life Equation	Pers./Prof. Framework	Personal Status (Record results)	Notes
☐ Insights to Success™—Interactive	a	b	c	d	e	f	g	h	i	j	k	l		
☐ Insights to Sales™—Interactive	a	b	c	d	e	f	g	h	i	j	k	l		
☐ Insights to Relationships™—Interactive	a	b	c	d	e	f	g	h	i	j	k	l		
☐ Managing for Success® (MFS)—Executive	a	b	c	d	e	f	g	h	i	j	k	l		
☐ MFS—Employee-Manager™	a	b	c	d	e	f	g	h	i	j	k	l		
☐ MFS—Sales	a	b	c	d	e	f	g	h	i	j	k	l		
☐ MFS—Work Environment™	a	b	c	d	e	f	g	h			k			
☐ MFS—Customer Service	a	b	c	d	e		g	h		j				
☐ MFS—Team Building	a	b	c	d	e		g							
☐ MFS—Personal Interests, Attitudes and Values™ (PIAV)	a	b	c	d	e	f	g	h	i	j	k	l		
☐ MFS—Interviewing Insights™—General	a	b	c	d	e									
☐ MFS—Interviewing Insights™—Sales	a	b	c	d	e									

ASSESSMENTS AND TOOLS

Target Training International (TTI)

☐ Assessment/Tool	Coaching	Attitude/Behavior	Change	Communication	Diversity	Performance	Teamwork	Technology	Time Management	Service	Work/Life Equation	Pers./Prof. Framework	PERSONAL STATUS (Record results)	NOTES
☐ MFS—Communicating with Style™	a	b	c	d	e	f	g			j	k	l		
☐ MFS—Time P.I.U.S.™	a	b	c	d	e	f	g		i	j	k	l		
☐ MFS—Sales Strategy Index™	a		c		e	f	g	h		j				
☐ Successful Career Planning™	a	b	c	d	e	f		h				l		
☐ Relationship Insights™	a	b	c	d	e		g			j	k	l		
☐ Golf Stroke Saver	a	b	c			f								
☐ Family Talk™—Parent/Young Adult	a	b	c	d	e						k	l		

ABOUT THE AUTHOR

D
r. Jylla Moore Foster, founder, president and chief executive officer of Crystal Stairs, Inc., is a nationally renowned business executive whose corporate, entrepreneurial, community, and coaching experiences have propelled her to the forefront of her field.

She specializes in leadership coaching and training for individuals, businesses, and organizations seeking to develop *conscious* and *intentional* leadership skills necessary to achieve personal, professional, and business goals. Her Leadership Assets™ program is based on the lessons learned coaching and training clients at several Fortune 500 firms and in organizations and academic institutions; as a former vice president at IBM, where she developed expertise in sales, marketing, operations, and technology; and as the twentieth international president of Zeta Phi Beta Sorority, a service organization of more than 100,000 women.

She earned her executive coaching certification from Corporate Coach University and is a member of the International Coach Federation (ICF) and the American Society for Training and Development (ASTD). Dr. Foster also holds a bachelor of science degree in mathematics from Livingstone College where she was a Samuel E. Duncan Scholar, and a master of business administration degree from Indiana University where she was a Consortium for Graduate Study Fellow. She was awarded an Honorary Doctor of Humane Letters in recognition of her professional achievements and community service by Livingstone College. In addition, she attended IBM's Harvard Business School's Client Executive Certification

Program, as well as the Center for Creative Leadership's training program.

Based on her professional expertise and extensive training, Dr. Foster helps executives, high-potential resources, and other leaders navigate through extraordinary challenges. Her passion as outlined in *Due North!* is to help them strengthen the Leadership Assets™ necessary for success in their personal and professional lives.

ABOUT
CRYSTAL STAIRS, INC.

C rystal Stairs, Inc. is a premier training, executive coaching, and consulting firm specializing in leadership development for individuals, corporations, educational institutions, government entities, and organizations. The firm offers leading-edge seminars, innovative coaching techniques, and *engaged speaking*™ presentations to help clients become focused, goal-oriented, results-driven, and successful in their work and life.

The firm's blue chip list of clients include such corporate giants as IBM, General Electric, Georgia-Pacific, and Value City Department Stores; professional associations such as the Information Technology Senior Management Forum (ITSMF), National Black MBA Association, and the National Association of African Americans in Human Resource Management; and several educational institutions, including Jackson State University, Savannah State University, and Livingstone College.

For further information about Crystal Stairs, please contact:

Crystal Stairs, Inc.
P. O. Box 157
Hinsdale, IL 60521

Tel: 630-734-1481
Fax: 630-734-1483

email: DueNorth@Crystal-Stairs.com
www.Crystal-Stairs.com

SUGGESTED READING

Books that have traveled with me on my life's journey . . . To each author, I am grateful!

Beech, Wendy. *Black Enterprise Guide to Starting Your Own Business.* New York: Wiley, 1999.

Bell, Ella, L. J. Edmondson, and Stella M. Nkomo. *Our Separate Ways: Black and White Women and the Struggle for Professional Identity.* Massachusetts: Harvard Business School Press, 2001.

Bonnstetter, Bill. *If I Knew Then What I Know Now.* New York: Forbes Custom Publishing, 1999.

Bonnstetter, Bill, Judy Suiter, and Randy Widrick. *The Universal Language DISC: A Reference Manual.* Arizona: Target Training International, 2001.

Boston, Kelvin. *Smart Money Moves for African Americans.* New York: Perigee, 1997.

Broussard, Cheryl D. *The Black Woman's Guide to Financial Independence: Smart Ways to Take Charge of Your Money, Build Wealth, and Achieve Financial Security.* New York: Penguin Books, 1996.

Brown, Les. *It's Not Over Until You Win!* New York: Simon & Schuster, 1997.

Cobbs, Dr. Price M.D., and Judith Turnock, Esq. *Cracking the Corporate Code: From Survival to Mastery.* Washington, DC: Executive Leadership Council, 2000.

Cole, Harriette. *How To Be: Contemporary Etiquette for African Americans.* New York: Simon & Schuster, 1999.

Coleman, Harvey. *Empowering Yourself: The Organizational Game Revealed.* Iowa: Kendall/Hunt Publishing Company, 1996.

Covey, Stephen R. *The Seven Habits of Highly Effective People.* New York: Simon & Schuster, 1989.

Ditzler, Jinny S. *Your Best Year Yet.* New York: Warner, 1994.

Edelman, Marian Wright. *The Measure of Our Success: A Letter to My Children and Yours.* Boston: Beacon Press, 1992.

Frankel, Dr. Lois. *JUMP-START Your Career: How the "STRENGTHS" that got you where you are today can hold you back tomorrow.* New York: Three Rivers Press, 1997.

Fraser, George. *Success Runs In Our Race. The Complete Guide to Effective Networking in the African-American Community.* New York: Avon Books, 1994.

Graves, Earl G. *How to Succeed in Business Without Being White: Straight Talk on Making It In America.* New York: HarperCollins Publishers, 1997.

Harrell, Keith. *Attitude Is Everything: 10 Life Changing Steps to Turning Attitude into Action.* New York: HarperCollins Publishers, 2000.

Hill, Hattie. *Smart Women, Smart Choices: Set Limits and Gain Control of Your Personal and Professional Life.* New York: Golden Books, 1998.

Holmes, Steven A. *Ron Brown: An Uncommon Life.* New York: Wiley, 2000.

Jenkins, Lee. *Taking Care of Business: Establishing A Financial Legacy for the African American Family.* Chicago: Moody Press, 2001.

Johnson, John H. *Succeeding Against the Odds.* New York: Warner, 1989.

Johnson, Dr. Spencer M.D. *Who Moved My Cheese?* New York: Putnam, 1998.

Jolley, Willie. *It Only Takes A Minute To Change Your Life!* New York: St. Martin's Press, 1997.

Kimbro, Dennis, Ph.D. *What Makes the Great Great.* New York: Doubleday, 1997.

King, Rev. Dr. Barbara. *Transform Your Life: From fear to faith. . . From loneliness to love. . . from self-doubt to self-discovery.* New York: Perigee, 1995.

Kiyosaki, Robert, with Sharon Lechter. *Rich Dad, Poor Dad: What The Rich Teach Their Kids About Money — That The Poor and Middle Class Do Not!* New York: Warner, 1998.

LaBelle, Patti, with Laura B. Randolph. *Don't Block the Blessings: Revelations of a Lifetime.* New York: Riverhead Books, 1996.

Lundin, Stephen, Ph.D., Harry Paul, and John Christensen. *FISH!: A Remarkable Way to Boost Morale and Improve Results.* New York: Hyperion, 2000.

Mandela, Nelson. *Long Walk to Freedom.* Canada: Little, Brown & Company, 1994.

Niemela, Cynder, and Rachael Lewis. *Leading High Impact Teams: The Coach Approach to Peak Performance.* California: High Impact Publishing, 2001.

Pagonis, Lt. General William G. *Moving Mountains: Lessons in Leadership and Logistics from the Gulf War.* Massachusetts: Harvard Business School Press, 1992.

Peters, Tom. *The Brand You 50: Reinventing Work.* New York: Alfred Knopf, 1999.

Powell, Colin L., with Joseph Persico. *My American Journey.* New York: Random House, 1995.

Poynter, Dan. *The Self-Publishing Manual: How to Write, Print and Sell Your Own Book.* California: Para Publishing, 2000.

Redfield, James. *The Celestine Prophecy.* New York: Warner, 1993.

Richardson, Cheryl. *Take Time for Your Life: A Personal Coach's 7-Step Program for Creating the Life You Want.* New York: Broadway Books, 1998.

Ritchey, Tom, with Alan Axelrod. *I'm Stuck, You're Stuck: Break Through to Better Work Relationships and Results by Discovering Your DiSC® Style.* California: Berrett-Koehler Publishers, 2002.

Ruiz, Don Miguel. *The Four Agreements.* California: Amber-Allen Publishing, 1997.

Russell-McCloud, Patricia. *A Is for Attitude: An Alphabet for Living.* New York: HarperCollins Publishers, 1999.

Schultz, Howard, and Dori Jones Yang. *Pour Your Heart Into It: How Starbucks Built a Company One Cup at a Time.* New York: Hyperion, 1997.

Senge, Peter M. *The Fifth Discipline. The Art & Practice of The Learning Organization.* New York: Doubleday, 1990.

Taylor, Susan. *In The Spirit.* New York: Amistad, 1993.

Tietelbaum, Daniel. *The Ultimate Guide to Mental Toughness: How to Raise your Motivation, Focus and Confidence Like Pushing a Button.* Maryland: Demblin Communications, 1998.

Weaver, Vanessa, Ph.D., and Jan Hill. *Smart Women Smart Moves.* New York: AMACOM, 1994.

Wilkinson, Bruce. *The Prayer of Jabez: Breaking Through to the Blessed Life.* Oregon: Multnomah Publishers, 2000.

Williams, Terrie. *The Personal Touch: What You Really Need to Succeed in Today's Fast-paced Business World.* New York: Warner, 1994.

PERMISSIONS

MapQuest® on page xi is a registered trademark of MapQuest.com, Inc. and is used with permission.

Excerpt from the Langston Hughes poem, "Mother to Son," from the book *The Collected Poems of Langston Hughes* on page 1, reprinted with permission from publisher, Alfred A. Knopf, a division of Random House.

The Coaching Checklist© on page 21 and Inside Out Shifts: A Coaching Model© on page 23, reprinted with permission from Dr. Lee Smith and Dr. Jeannine Sandstrom of CoachWorks® International.

The Attitude Assessment on page 29, permission granted by Keith Harrell, president of Harrell Performance Systems, Inc.

The Attitudes and Values summary on page 30, permission granted by Bill Bonnstetter, founder and president of Target Training International, Ltd.

Personal Profile Classical Patterns One Line Descriptions on pages 36-37, reprinted with permission from Don Cipriano of Cipriano Training and Development.

Quote by Susan L. Taylor on page 41, reprinted with permission from Susan L. Taylor, sr. vice president and editorial director, *Essence* Magazine.

Tips on electronic communication on page 56, permission granted by Judy Irving, courage coach, Moving On.

Certified Communicator Program on pages 57-59, permission granted by Sheri Ross, Coach U.

The Performance, Image, and Exposure Success Formula on page 83, reprinted with permission from Harvey Coleman, president and CEO of Coleman Management Consultants, Inc.

Derailment Factors on page 83, permission granted by Lois P. Frankel, Ph.D., Corporate Coaching International.

The Top 10 High Impact Team Practices on pages 93–94, reprinted with permission from Rachael Lewis, principal, Trilogy Coaching Institute and Cynder Niemela, managing partner, VISTA COACH.

Quote by Benjamin Mays on page 109, reprinted with permission from *Quotable Quotes* © 1983 by Dr. Benjamin Mays, published by Vantage Press.

The story, "Standing Up on the Inside" on page 135, reprinted with permission from Pastor's Story File.

Tips for Success That Guarantee You Will Stand Out Over Everyone Else on pages 142–143, permission granted by Terrie M. Williams, founder, The Stay Strong Foundation, and The Terrie Williams Agency.

DiSC® and other assessments so designated in the book are registered trademarks of Inscape Publishing, Inc. and are used with permission.

Managing for Success® and other assessments so designated in the book are registered trademarks of Target Training International Ltd. and are used with permission.

LET US HEAR FROM YOU!

There are many stories to be told that individuals have experienced along their leadership journey. *Due North!* is the first book in a series that will share lessons learned related to the 12 Leadership Assets™. Crystal Stairs would like to publish your story along with additional reference information in subsequent volumes. We invite you to share your story for future publication.

Please send a copy of your story, quotes, suggested reading, assessments, web sites, or other related resources to:

Crystal Stairs, Inc.
P. O. Box 157
Hinsdale, IL 60521
Tel: 630-734-1481
Fax: 630-734-1483

email: DueNorth@Crystal-Stairs.com
Visit us at: www.Crystal-Stairs.com

Please include with your submission contact information including name, mailing address, phone number, and email address. It would also be helpful if you specified the Leadership Asset most aligned with your information.

Thank you for sharing as we continue to *Strengthen Leadership Assets*™!

INDEX